NATIONAL ISSUES FORUMS

I n theory, democratic government rests on the idea of popular sovereignty. Writing in 1798, James Madison envisioned an informed electorate actively participating in public policy debates. In practice, of course, democratic government doesn't often work that way. "The notion that the public really controls the government," writes columnist Anthony Lewis, "has always had elements of myth in it."

The recent presidential election campaign was widely regarded as an unsatisfying process, which often veered away from the matter of how the country should be governed toward highly personal questions about who would govern it. Some pressing national issues were barely addressed. Finding the whole process boring and irrelevant, many people have simply dropped out of electoral politics.

This sense of alienation from the electoral process is a symptom of deeper dissatisfactions with the democratic process, which have as much to do with our role as citizens as they do with how campaigns are run, or the actions of elected officials. It is not enough for us to sit in front of our televisions, watching political campaigns and listening to elected officials. Democracy is not, after all, a spectator sport.

As James Madison reminded his readers, a working democracy assumes that citizens are *active* participants. But participants in what, exactly? For the majority of us who do not hold public office, it is not clear how we can participate in public life, other than casting a vote and paying taxes. In many communities, no forums are held at which people discuss public issues.

The purpose of the National Issues Forums (NIF) — locally initiated Forums and study circles which bring citizens together in communities across the nation for nonpartisan discussion about public issues — is to provide a place for the practice of citizenship. In several respects, the NIF is intended to restore what's missing from the democratic process.

Since the word "citizen" is often used rhetorically, it may seem odd to think of the citizen's role as one that requires specific skills that have to be cultivated, like other skills. Yet the premise of the NIF is that the skills of public discourse — listening as well as talking about common problems and comparing different views of the public interest — are as important today as they were in the eighteenth century, when town meetings were a vital public institution.

Each year, convenors of NIF choose three issues for discussion. Since good talk requires a common framework and a certain familiarity with the issue, a book like this one is prepared for each topic. A distinctive feature of these books is that they present several choices. Citizens need to put themselves in the position of elected officials by considering various courses of action, and learning about their costs and consequences. An important aspect of what we refer to as "choicework" is to examine how our values as individuals and community members apply to a particular issue.

After the community Forums and study groups meet, the NIF convenes a series of meetings with national leaders to convey the outcome of these discussions. So that we can convey your thoughts and feelings about this issue, two ballots are included at the end of this book. Before you begin reading these materials and then after you've read them and taken part in Forums, I urge you to fill them out and mail them back to us.

This book, like the others in this series, is a guide to one of the nation's pressing issues and an invitation to engage in public discussion about it.

Keith Melville

Keith Melville, Editor-in-Chief

Editor-in-Chief: Keith Melville
Writer: Keith Melville
Research: Sophie Rosenfeld
Editor: Betty Frecker
Ballots: John Doble, Josh Klein, and
    Amy Richardson
Production Manager:
    George Cavanaugh
Production Director: Robert E. Daley

Designer: Sundberg, Morance &
    Associates Inc.
Circulation Coordinator:
    Victoria Simpson
Cover Illustration: Niculae Asciu
Word Processing: Valerie Braum
Formatting: Karen Bocko
Graphic Research: Sophie Rosenfeld

The books in this series are prepared by The Public Agenda Foundation — a nonprofit, nonpartisan organization devoted to research and education about public issues — and published jointly by the Kettering Foundation and the Kendall/Hunt Publishing Company. They are used by civic and educational organizations interested in addressing public issues.

In particular, they are used in local discussion groups that are part of a nationwide network, the National Issues Forums (NIF). The NIF consists of more than 1,300 civic and educational organizations — colleges and universities, libraries, service clubs, and membership groups. Although each community group is locally controlled, NIF is a collaborative effort. Each year, convenors choose three issues and use common materials — issue books such as this one, and parallel audio and videotape materials.

Groups interested in using the NIF materials and adapting its approach as part of their own program are invited to write or call for further information: National Issues Forums, 100 Commons Road, Dayton, Ohio 45459-2777. Phone 1-800-433-7834, in Ohio dial 1-800-433-4819.

The NIF issue books— both the standard edition and an abridged version at a lower reading level, as well as audiocassette and videocassette versions of the same material — can be ordered from Kendall/Hunt Publishing Company, 2460 Kerper Boulevard, Dubuque, Iowa 52004-0539. Phone 1-800-338-5578. The following titles are available:

The Day Care Dilemma: Who Should Be Responsible for the Children?
The Drug Crisis: Public Strategies for Breaking the Habit
The Environment at Risk: Responding to Growing Dangers
Health Care for the Elderly: Moral Dilemmas, Mortal Choices
Coping with AIDS: The Public Response to the Epidemic
The Public Debt: Breaking the Habit of Deficit Spending
The Superpowers: Nuclear Weapons and National Security
The Trade Gap: Regaining the Competitive Edge
Freedom of Speech: Where to Draw the Line
Crime: What We Fear, What Can Be Done
Immigration: What We Promised, Where to Draw the Line
The Farm Crisis: Who's in Trouble, How to Respond

ISBN 0-8403-5264-6

THE DAY CARE DILEMMA: WHO SHOULD BE RESPONSIBLE FOR THE CHILDREN?

PREPARED BY THE PUBLIC AGENDA FOUNDATION

CONTENTS

THE CHILD CARE DEBATE: PARENTS' NEEDS, PUBLIC COMMITMENTS

"Broad concern about how to help parents of preschoolers juggle work and family responsibilities has sparked intense debate. What should government provide? What should families be expected to do on their own?"

After years as a political wallflower, child care has recently emerged as a prominent item on the public agenda. During the 1988 presidential campaign, both candidates spent as much time at day care centers as they did at traditional campaign stops such as factory gates and county fairs. Judging by the number of times George Bush and Michael Dukakis were photographed surrounded by preschoolers, it appeared that 4-year-olds were expected to cast a decisive vote.

One reason candidates scheduled so many photo opportunities at day care centers was to humanize their images by showing that they could lead preschoolers in a rousing chorus of "Itsy Bitsy Spider." A more important reason is that since record numbers of mothers are in the labor force, child care is a matter of immediate personal concern to millions of voters.

On Capitol Hill, Democrats and Republicans alike have tried to claim family policy as their domain. Senator Edward Kennedy recently called for "a major program of national investment in our children, equivalent to the Marshall Plan of the 1940s or the mission to the moon in the 1960s." On the other side of the aisle, Senator Orrin Hatch, one of the more conservative members of the Senate, was just as vociferous. "The question of to whom we entrust our children is one we have to face, lest we put a developmental, intellectual, and emotional mortgage on the next generation of Americans."

Beyond the question of what's good for young children, many people are concerned about the social consequences of neglecting their needs. At the state level, the National Governors' Association has called for renewed attention to child care and preschool education to give children a good start, to keep them from falling behind in school and eventually becoming unemployable.

To others, child care is an economic issue. As Governor Carroll Campbell, Jr. said in his 1989 message to the South Carolina legislature, "Lack of affordable day care constitutes one of the greatest obstacles for working women in South Carolina."

Concern about children's issues isn't limited to the public sector. In 1987, the Committee for Economic Development, a group of corporate executives, issued a report entitled *Children in Need.* Responding to concern about America's ability to compete in the global economy, the executives who prepared that report came out strongly in favor of increased assistance to families from business and government, including expanded funding for preschool programs.

The urgency of unmet needs, as well as broadly shared concern about how to help dual wage-earner parents juggle family and work responsibilities has sparked intense debate about child care. In the words of former Secretary of Labor Ann McLaughlin, "The issue of child care is politically ripe."

The child care debate raises fundamental questions about what is best for young children, what families should be expected to do on their own, and what the government's role should be.

LEAVE IT TO BEAVER'S MOTHER

If the children's cause is back on the public agenda, it was conspicuously absent for several decades. More so than in other industrial nations, child rearing in the United States has been regarded almost entirely as a private responsibility. Only under exceptional circumstances has the government been involved in child care. During the depression of the 1930s, for example, the federal government created several thousand nursery schools to provide jobs for unemployed teachers and to help parents employed by the Works Progress Administration.

During World War II, under the Lanham Act, the federal government provided day care facilities and nursery schools so mothers could work in war-related industries. At the Kaiser shipyard in Portland, Oregon, for example, centers were open 24 hours a day, 6 days a week, to provide health services for young children as well as day care. When the war ended, the Kaiser shipyard closed — and so did the Lanham centers. As Gilbert Steiner remarks in *The Children's Cause*, the Lanham Act was a "win-the-war program, not a save-the-children program."

When the soldiers came home after the war, most women left the workplace and returned home to care for their children. In the 1950s and early 1960s — the era of "Leave It To Beaver" families — public sentiment strongly opposed working mothers, and there was little discussion of the government's role in child care.

It wasn't until the mid-1960s, when the federal Head Start program was created, that child care programs and preschool education attracted much attention. Head Start was designed to help disadvantaged children. It was also intended to help low-income parents get off the welfare rolls. Though Head Start programs emphasized child development and education — not just custodial care — most Americans continued to regard day care as a service for welfare mothers, not something that middle-class parents wanted or that their children needed.

A few years later, however, child care advocates, feminists, and supporters of

programs for the disadvantaged formed a coalition to lobby on behalf of the boldest child care initiative of the postwar years, the Comprehensive Child Development Act of 1971.

The Act called for an ambitious program that would have expanded Head Start, provided $50 million for the creation of new child care facilities, and permitted further tax deductions for parents who used child care services. The legislation would have given millions of parents the option of placing their two-and-a-half-year-olds — and, under certain circumstances, even younger children — in publicly subsidized facilities offering education, nutrition, and health programs. For poor families, those services would have been free. Middle-class families would have paid according to their income. In brief, the Comprehensive

Child Development Act of 1971 proposed a broad commitment to day care and a well-defined public role.

In September 1971, despite strong opposition — Senator James Allen of Alabama said the proposal was evidence that America was "rapidly shaping up as a socialist society under an authoritarian government," and Senator James Buckley of New York charged that it would make the federal government the "arbiter of child rearing practices" — the Senate approved the Act by a substantial margin.

Later, the House approved the measure by the narrow margin of 186-183, despite strong opposition. Congressman Schmitz of California said that "A nation of orphanages cannot endure, and should not." By November, when the House voted, the bill was

NICULAE ASCIU

5

IT'S 9:00 A.M. ON A TYPICAL WORKDAY . . .
WHAT ARRANGEMENTS HAVE BEEN MADE FOR THE PRESCHOOLERS?

In the United States, there are roughly 20 million children under the age of 6. The mothers of about 10.5 million of those children are in the labor force. The chief factors influencing parents' choices about child care arrangements are the child's age, the availability of care and its cost, and their judgment about what kind of care is best for the child.

The three main options for families in which the mother does not stay home to care for young children are home care, family day care, and organized day care:

- *Care Provided in the Child's Home:* Roughly one-quarter of young children whose parents work full time are cared for in their homes by a nanny, housekeeper, *au pair*, or baby-sitter — an arrangement that is convenient and expensive unless a relative serves as caretaker.

- *Family Day Care:* The most common arrangement for infants and children under 3 years old is care in another person's home, or family day care. Though about 25 percent of family day care is provided by relatives, 75 percent is care given by nonrelatives. Typically, while caring for her own young child, a woman is paid by neighbors to take care of their toddlers in her home.

- *Day Care Centers:* Organized day care centers, which usually serve 10 or more children in a facility arranged for this purpose, are especially popular for 3- and 4-year-olds.

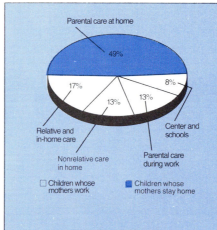

Parental care at home 49%
17% 8%
13% 13%
Relative and in-home care
Center and schools
Nonrelative care in home
Parental care during work
☐ Children whose mothers work   ■ Children whose mothers stay home

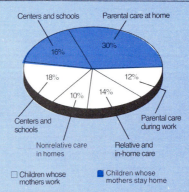

Centers and schools 16%   Parental care at home 30%
18% 12%
10% 14%
Centers and schools
Parental care during work
Nonrelative care in homes
Relative and in-home care
☐ Children whose mothers work   ■ Children whose mothers stay home

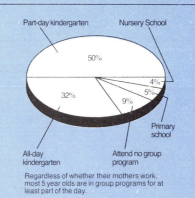

Part-day kindergarten 50%   Nursery School
4%
5%
32% 9%
All-day kindergarten
Attend no group program
Primary school

Regardless of whether their mothers work, most 5 year olds are in group programs for at least part of the day.

BIRTH TO 2-YEAR-OLDS

Many infants and toddlers are cared for in home settings, either by relatives or nonrelatives.

Major concerns: Many family day care facilities are unlicensed, and some provide inadequate supervision. Since infants require more attention, the cost of day care for infants is often higher — in many cases, more than parents can afford. In most communities, the demand for infant day care far exceeds the supply.

THREE- AND FOUR-YEAR-OLDS

Although several states are considering prekindergarten programs for all 4-year-olds, public programs for such children are currently provided only to children from poor families. Head Start primarily serves this age group.

Major concerns: Many programs are part day. Private facilities are often too expensive for low- and middle-income families.

FIVE-YEAR-OLDS

All states provide kindergarten programs for 5-year-olds, and 5 states *require* attendance in kindergarten for children of this age.

Major concerns: Many kindergarten programs are half day, requiring working parents to make other arrangements for the remainder of the day.

> "A quiet revolution has taken place in the American family, which has transformed the way in which families function and children are raised."

sharply criticized by groups that regarded it as an attack on family values.

Finally, President Nixon reversed his earlier position and vetoed the legislation, saying that it would lead to the breakdown of the American family. "For the federal government to plunge headlong financially into supporting child development," the president said, "would commit the vast moral authority of the government to the side of communal approaches to child rearing over against the family-centered approach." For years afterward, the firestorm of opposition to the bill dampened congressional interest in child care legislation.

THE QUIET REVOLUTION

Over the past several decades, a quiet revolution has taken place in the American family, which has transformed the way in which families function and children are raised. In 1950, only 12 percent of married women with children under 6 had jobs outside the home. At the time, three out of four adults disapproved of married women who worked in the labor force if they didn't have to. Working mothers were made to feel guilty. They were reproached with truisms: even a bad mother, it was said, is better than good day care.

Child rearing experts contributed to the emphasis on full-time mothering. In the first edition of Benjamin Spock's *Baby and Child Care,* published in 1945 — and in every revision until the 1980s — Spock equated proper child care with mothering, and described mothering as a full-time job.

The first edition of Spock's book was written at a time when considerable attention was devoted to problems that arise from inadequate mothering, a subject researchers explored in studies

Family day care is one of the most popular forms of child care.

of institutionalized children. Researchers noted that children who were brought up in orphanages and deprived of normal mothering — especially during the first two or three years of life — tend to be emotionally withdrawn, and are subsequently unable to form close attachments. That research led some psychologists to conclude that all young children need the continuous attention of their mothers.

The British psychoanalyst John Bowlby was influential in focusing attention on what he called maternal deprivation. In a book entitled *Child Care and the Growth of Love,* Bowlby commented on the effect of parental care on the child's development: "What is believed to be essential for mental health," he wrote, "is that an infant and young child should experience a warm, intimate, and continuous relationship with the mother (or permanent mother-substitute)."

When Bowlby asserted the "absolute need of infants and toddlers for the continuous care of their mothers," many mothers must have wondered if they could stray from the child's side. For them, Bowlby offered this advice: "Leaving any child under three years of age is a major operation to be undertaken only for good reasons, and when undertaken, planned with great care."

Although Bowlby's concern about the effects of separating mothers from their young children during the day is shared by many, it has also been strongly challenged. As one writer Rochelle Wortis put it, Bowlby's conclusions represent "a dangerously unscientific extrapolation from studies of institutionalized children to the more common situation in which infants leave their homes for part of the day, are cared for by other responsible adults, and are returned again to their homes."

RICK REINHARD

If children need constant attention from their mothers, we have a serious problem, for many of them do not get it. In one of the most dramatic changes of the past four decades, the percentage of married women with children under 6 who work in the labor force increased from 12 percent in 1950 to 57 percent in 1987. Of the 10 million children under 6 who have working mothers, two-thirds have mothers who work full time.

The increase in working mothers whose children are less than three years of age is especially dramatic. Until 1975 the Census Bureau did not even collect labor force data on mothers with young children because it assumed that few such mothers worked. The most recent figures show that more than half of the mothers of children under two work in the labor force. In fact, Census statistics show that by 1988 more than half of all mothers with children under age 1 —

50.8 percent — were in the job market, either part or full time.

Compared to the 1950s, when working mothers were made to feel guilty, the shoe is now on the other foot. Because three out of four adults approve of women who choose to work in the labor force, married women who would prefer not to work in the labor force often feel considerable pressure to do so. A recent *New York Times*/CBS News Poll suggests that, at least among people who are under thirty, 75 percent think that married women *should* work, whether or not they have children.

The clearest indication of how far we have come from the child-rearing practices of the postwar period is that only about one-fourth of all married couples with children are families in which the wife stays home as a full-time mother. Moreover, there has been a dramatic increase in the number of single-parent households.

Whereas only one in ten children in 1970 lived in a one-parent family, that figure is now closer to one in five.

TAKING CARE OF THE CHILDREN

The rapid entry of married women into the labor force over the past few decades has fundamentally altered the way in which young children are raised. As recently as 1971, when President Nixon vetoed the Comprehensive Child Care Act, day care was still widely regarded as a necessary evil, to be avoided if at all possible. Polls taken at the time showed that the public was deeply divided about whether to encourage child care provided outside the home by someone other than relatives.

Since then, resistance to paid day care has faded. The people who most strongly favor facilities of this sort, according to a Roper poll, are parents who are single, divorced, or separated — which is not surprising, considering their dependence upon organized day care. Significantly, however, many parents are now convinced that out-of-home care is not harmful to children, and that good day care programs are good for children. Partly because of the widely shared view among parents and child development specialists that group experiences are important for early development, participation in a child care program is an increasingly common experience for young children, whether their mothers are in the labor force or not.

Adjusting to the new realities of family life has required wholesale changes in American life. Take-out food services are booming. Housekeeping standards have relaxed. Dual wage-earner families practice "tag-team parenting." The growing ranks of single or divorced parents struggle to

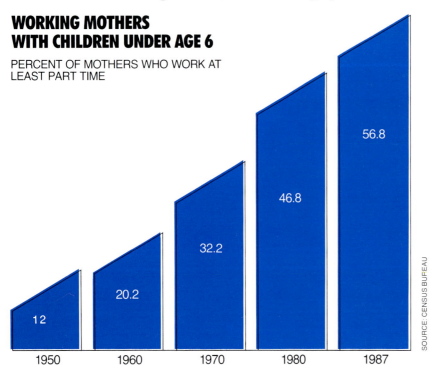

WORKING MOTHERS WITH CHILDREN UNDER AGE 6

PERCENT OF MOTHERS WHO WORK AT LEAST PART TIME

1950	1960	1970	1980	1987
12	20.2	32.2	46.8	56.8

SOURCE: CENSUS BUREAU

"The debate over parental leave raises this question: should employers be required to provide certain benefits to new parents?"

PARENTAL LEAVE

While the child care debate focuses on what *government* should do for families with young children the debate over parental leave raises questions about what *employers* should do — and the circumstances under which government should require employers to provide certain benefits.

Currently, the only federal law pertaining to maternity leave is the Pregnancy Discrimination Act of 1978, which requires that health conditions related to pregnancy be treated like other short-term disabilities. If an employer provides disability benefits, the law requires that pregnant women must be eligible for them.

Consequently, many firms pay a new mother's wages for the period she is unable to work — typically six to eight weeks — and guarantee job security over that period. However, because roughly half of all American companies provide no disability coverage, it is estimated that about 50 percent of working women do not qualify for maternity benefits.

By equating maternity leave with other short-term disabilities, the 1978 law was narrowly concerned with the *physical* effects of pregnancy and childbirth. Advocates of parental leave insist that it is equally important to recognize the *psychological* needs of parents and infants in the first few months of the child's life. Over the past few years, support has grown for the position that job-protected leave, with partial pay, should be available to new parents.

As things stand, employers decide whether or not to offer parental leave to facilitate the parent's adjustment to the infant. A growing number of companies permit unpaid parental leave — for new fathers as well as mothers — for several months. Southern New England Bell, for example, guarantees the employee's job for a period of up to six months of unpaid parental leave. This allows mothers to choose to stay home for several months after the period covered by maternity leave; it also permits a father to stay home for several months after a child is born. However, policies of this type are

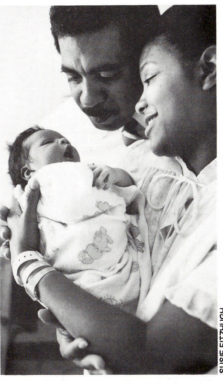

SUSIE FITZHUGH

the exception rather than the rule, which is why parental leave has become an increasingly prominent issue.

Proponents point out that many mothers are obliged to return to the labor forces soon after the birth of their babies. No matter how much they might prefer to take several months off to get acquainted with the new baby, mothers face the loss of their jobs, or their seniority, if they do so.

The United States is the only industrial nation that does not guarantee parents the right to spend time with newborns without jeopardizing their jobs. Most European countries provide leaves for infant care of several months, with benefits averaging more than 50 percent of the woman's normal wage.

Proposals along those lines are being considered in several states and in Congress. So far, however, only a few such proposals have actually gone into effect. In Connecticut, as of July 1988, all state employees are entitled to 24 weeks of family leave within a 2-year period, upon the birth or adoption of a child, or the serious illness of a child.

In Congress, Connecticut Senator Christopher Dodd is one of the sponsors of a bill that would require employers to provide unpaid leave of up to ten weeks over two years for employees who need to attend to family needs in case of childbirth, adoption, or serious illness.

Although the bill was defeated in the Senate in October 1988, it will almost certainly be reconsidered. Proponents of a national parental leave policy such as Representative Marge Roukema insist that requiring companies to provide for parental leave is "completely consistent with traditional labor laws" such as minimum wage and safety rules.

But many businesses are adamantly opposed to federal laws that establish costly new regulations. Alexander Trowbridge, president of the National Association of Manufacturers, said that a parental leave requirement would force employers to reduce other employee benefits. Particular concern has been expressed about the burden such measures impose on small firms that do not have adequate resources to hire and train part-time replacements for employees who are on leave.

meet the dual demands of providing financial and emotional support for their children. Parents patch together arrangements for their young children by calling on grandparents or babysitters, hiring illegal aliens as nannies, organizing nurseries, and scouting nearby day care facilities.

In 1950, when only 12 percent of mothers with children under 6 were in the labor force, families could meet most of their child care needs by themselves, occasionally calling on relatives or neighbors for assistance. Today, however, because a majority of mothers of children under age 6 are in the labor force — many of them in full-time employment — parents and relatives are able to provide care for only about half of the children who need it.

Consequently, demand for organized day care programs has soared. According to a study by the Center for Policy Research in Education, the rate of preschool enrollment for 3- and 4-year-olds has almost doubled over the past 15 years.

A PATCHWORK SYSTEM

Responding to that demand, the day care industry has expanded dramatically. Facilities range from "mom and pop"-operated play schools to nationwide operations like Kinder-Care, whose brightly colored facilities are almost as common in many parts of the country as the golden arches of McDonald's.

Across the country, employer-sponsored child care programs are increasingly common. Over the past decade, according to the Work and Family Information Center at The Conference Board, a business research organization in New York, the number of U.S. firms that provide some form of child care assistance — financial assistance for child care, alternative work schedules, or child care centers located at or near the work site — has increased from about 100 to more than 3,000.

Though the private sector is becoming more involved, the majority of employers has not responded. Most parents rely on limited support from the federal government. It continues to

fund the Head Start program, and it provides subsidies for day care centers and other child care services for low-income children through the Social Service Block Grant program, known as Title XX.

Growing awareness that middle-income families also struggle with child care prompted Congress to pass the child care tax credit in 1976 — which currently provides a subsidy of almost $4 billion a year to about 4 million families.

Throughout the 1980s, the states have been more directly involved in child care than the federal government. A majority of states now has special advisory commissions on children and families, and several states have exemplary programs. Massachusetts was one of the first states to devise a comprehensive child care system. California provides a child care information and referral service, which puts parents in touch with nearby family day care mothers, after-school programs, and day care centers. Minnesota has adopted the most progressive child care tax credit in the nation.

Evidence that preschool programs enhance later learning has prompted growing — if still modest — state support for early childhood programs, particularly prekindergarten programs.

Still, advocates of expanded public child care point out that the overall picture is not so bright. Despite growing demand for child care, 29 states have cut back funds for child care since 1981. For all the concern at the state level about child care, state coffers are not deep enough to meet the need.

Across the country, many working parents have discovered that quality child care is hard to find and difficult to afford. Despite public subsidies for child care, parents still pay the bulk of the child care bill, which averages

CATHY BLAIVAS

$3,000 a year for full-time day care. Even those who can afford to pay often have difficulty finding adequate facilities. Parents of infants have a particularly difficult time finding satisfactory arrangements. In most communities, the demand for infant care substantially exceeds the supply. Currently, the child care "system" in the United States is a patchwork, and one that is widely regarded as inadequate to the needs of parents as well as children. As indicated in a 1988 poll conducted by Marttila and Kiley, three-fourths of the American public says that it is difficult for parents to find affordable, good-quality child care.

GOVERNMENT'S ROLE

What should be done regarding day care? Few people would quarrel with the assertion George Bush made in his first congressional address as president, that child care "is one of the most important issues facing the nation."

But when it comes to specific proposals, such as the administration's proposal for tax credits to help low-income families with child care — the first major legislative initiative of the Bush administration — there is no consensus about what should be done.

Judging from the fact that Congress is considering dozens of bills with child care provisions, there appears to be considerable support for expanded federal efforts to assist families with young children. The initiatives under consideration in Congress — like the child care proposals that have been introduced in state legislatures — reflect a variety of views about how to help American families. Some would provide tax relief to assist mothers who stay home with young children. Others would expand Head Start-type programs for the disadvantaged or subsidize day care for low and moder-

HOW IMPORTANT DO YOU THINK THE ISSUE OF CHILD CARE IS IN THIS CAMPAIGN?

MODERATOR

ETTA HULME, *THE FORT WORTH STAR-TELEGRAM*

ate-income families. Yet others focus on improving the quality of child care programs.

Some people feel that the most promising course of action is to put more of the burden of responding to the needs of families with young children on corporations. To encourage working parents to spend more time with newborns and infants, Congress is considering a proposal that would require employers to offer longer parental leave. More than 30 states have introduced legislation to require parental leave. Across the country, there is active consideration of additional incentives to corporations to provide assistance with child care.

These proposals are being considered at a time when federal spending programs are severely constrained, when business is trying to control benefit costs in the face of worldwide competition, and when opinion polls show that the public's desire for social services is exceeded only by its reluctance to pay higher taxes. In one respect, the question is what Americans are willing to pay — either in

higher taxes or consumer costs — to help families cope with new demands.

FUNDAMENTAL QUESTIONS

Before asking how much government should do for preschoolers and their families, however, some fundamental questions need to be addressed. We need to talk first about what is best for young children and their parents, about the government's role and its limits, and about what services people should be entitled to regardless of their means.

The parents of a significant fraction of America's preschoolers already use organized day care, either because it permits mothers to work or because day care is regarded as an enriching experience, or both. The debate begins with the question of whether day care is in the best interest of children. Should the trend toward child care provided outside the home by someone other than parents or relatives be encouraged?

"Before day care becomes locked in

as an accepted fact of contemporary American life," writes Joan Beck, a syndicated columnist and author of several books on child development, "it deserves much more critical examination and debate. Doubts and criticism should not be brushed off as efforts to push women out of the workplace and back into second-class status."

If day care *is* in the best interests of children, another question needs to be raised: Should it continue to be primarily the family's responsibility or should government assist families to a greater extent? Some people conclude that existing arrangements are generally satisfactory and that there is no reason for government to take a larger role.

Currently, child care services are provided at public expense only to "at-risk" children — and only to some of them. The government provides a tax credit for families using child care. Beyond that, however, there is no public commitment to assist with child care. This is still essentially a private matter. It is up to parents to decide whether day care is in the child's best interest, to make arrangements, and to pay for them.

Some people insist that the assumption that parents should provide for the needs of preschoolers, without much public assistance, is increasingly unrealistic. In the words of Edward Zigler, a child development expert who was influential in forming the Head Start program, "Asking people to solve this on their own is like asking people in the late nineteenth century to set up and pay for their own schools. It just doesn't make any sense. It's a public problem that society must address."

If government subsidies make sense, should they be available to all parents

with young children, or are subsidies appropriate only for low-income families? Criticizing the patchwork child care system that has evolved over the past several decades, Alfred Kahn and Sheila Kamerman of the Columbia University School of Social Work assert that "The time has come for society — and for state and federal government — to acknowledge child care as a major need and to regard participation in child care as normative. Child care should become as much a part of the social infrastructure as libraries, parks, and highways. Child care should be regarded as an entitlement, like schools."

But this is by no means a view that commands universal support. Currently, there is no consensus that children should be entitled to day care, subsidized at public expense and made available to all families, regardless of income.

CHOICES AND CONSEQUENCES

This book explores these questions by examining the pros and cons of three perspectives on child care:

Choice #1 is based on the conviction that child care for preschoolers is not in their best interest, nor is it beneficial to American society over the long run. The government should support a traditional mothering role for women, because it is the best way to encourage the physical and emotional development of children. Subsidies for child care insidiously undermine the family by encouraging mothers of young children to enter the labor force. Inadequate income and high taxes have driven women into the workplace to supplement family income. From this perspective, the goal of public policy should be to reduce the financial burden on families, to make it possible for one parent to stay home to rear young children.

Choice #2 is based on the premise that there is a clear role for government in day care, but only for children who are at risk. The government has always responded to children in distress, such as those who are abandoned, abused, or neglected. For the same reason, early childhood programs for children from poor families are in the public interest. Quality early childhood programs for disadvantaged children lead to greater success in school, as well as the labor market. Proponents of this choice conclude that an expanded day care program for such children represents a sound social investment because it is a promising way to break the cycle of poverty.

Choice #3 rests on the assertion that the federal government should play an important role in guaranteeing that *all* families with young children have access to affordable, high-quality day care. Currently, because of the high cost of good child care services, many parents resort to makeshift arrangements. A pro-family policy has to take into consideration the needs of working parents as well as their children. Adequate child care arrangements for preschoolers from all types of families are essential if women are expected to be wage earners and to pursue careers on an equal basis with men.

Each of these choices involves certain costs — either a burden that falls on individual families or the cost of expanded public initiatives. But the debate over day care is far more than a discussion of what government can afford. In a deeper sense, it is a discussion about the government's role and its limits, and what families should be expected to do on their own. It is a discussion about what is in the best interest of America's children and families. ■

CHOICE #1
THE PRO-FAMILY SOLUTION: WHAT PARENTS DO BEST

"Surrogate care for preschoolers is not in their best interest, nor is it beneficial to society over the long run. Government should take measures to help more mothers raise preschoolers at home."

For all the ways in which the presidential candidates in Campaign '88 disagreed, they agreed that American parents need more help in raising small children, and both candidates proposed child care plans. George Bush called child care "nothing short of a family necessity," and proposed tax credits to help defray the cost of day care. For his part, Michael Dukakis declared in his acceptance speech that it is "time to see that young families are never again forced to choose between the jobs they need and the children they need." He endorsed start-up funding for the Act for Better Child Care, a comprehensive proposal to provide funding for day care.

Both candidates seemed to favor the long-term objective defined by Edward Zigler, that "every child should have equal access to child care." In Zigler's words, "The child care solution must cover the child from as early in pregnancy as possible through at least the first 12 years of life."

However, proponents of this first perspective on child care are convinced that by talking about solutions before we agree upon the problem, we're likely to end up with public policy that is seriously misguided. As they see it, the underlying problem isn't that there are too few day care facilities, or that they are too expensive for many parents to afford. Rather, the problem is that the rising cost of living and raising children — and rising levels of taxation — have forced many mothers into the workplace. Consequently, an increasing number of young children spend the day in child care programs while their parents work.

Day care, say critics, is a dehumanizing experience.

Rather than encouraging mothers to join the labor force by subsidizing day care programs, government should concentrate on ways to make staying home economically feasible. Instead of encouraging greater reliance on non-maternal care, government should take measures to permit more mothers to raise children at home.

"However unintentionally," said former Secretary of Education William Bennett in congressional hearings in April 1988, "the child care proposals now pending before Congress put families to one side. They seem to accept as inevitable the declining importance and role of the family. They seem more concerned with creating new [day care] structures than with supporting the best possible situation for our children."

In brief, advocates of this position are convinced that public policy should encourage families to be families. To defend this choice, proponents feel, is not to try to turn the clock back, nor to deny mothers of young children the right to jobs and careers. It is, rather, to put first things first: to insist that child care policy must be based upon what is best for children, not what is most convenient for their parents.

PARENTAL CARE

The premise of this position is that there is no substitute for the care parents provide for their own children. Government-subsidized day care is not in the best interest of children, says writer and social critic George Gilder, because no one else can supply "the love and attention that mothers spontaneously offer their children."

Few people doubt the importance of nurturing small children. The consistent care that mothers have traditionally provided is especially important in the first three years of life. These are the years when character is formed and when the crucial process of emotional attachment occurs. Since secure attachment in infancy and early childhood is the basis for self-regulation, independence, and the capacity for mature interdependence, deficiencies in the early years often lead to serious problems later on.

Experts generally agree that close and continuous contact between parents and children early in life is clearly in the child's best interest. It is also a matter of fundamental importance for society as a whole. "High-quality mother care strengthens society," says Phyllis Schlafly, "by

Phyllis Schlafly and her "Baby Buggy Brigade" picketing in Washington in favor of tax breaks for mothers of young children.

providing young children with the foundation on which to learn the basic skills necessary to be good citizens, cultured people, and productive workers. Constant and reliable supervision reduces the chances of juvenile delinquency and adolescent pregnancy, and improves the likelihood that children will finish high school and go on to further education."

How is day care different from parental care? Often, professional care givers are women of childbearing age and many are well trained. In general, it is not the absence of experienced child care providers that distinguishes paid care. The difference between the two is the emotional investment, the fact that no one else loves the child in the same way, or provides as much patient attention.

Advocates of this view stress that there is no substitute — at any price — for parental care. "The truth about paid child-rearing," says policy analyst and columnist Karl Zinsmeister, "is that it is rarely more than a weak stand-in for parental care. Someone is being asked to do for money what very few of us are able to do for any reason other than love."

The hallmarks of exceptional child care, as Zinsmeister notes, are small acts, endlessly repeated — such as "giving a reason why rather than just saying no; rewarding a small triumph with a joyful expression; risking a tantrum to correct a small habit that could be overlooked but would be better resolved; showering unqualified devotion."

For this reason, concludes Zinsmeister, "It will always be extremely difficult — no matter what laws or subsidies prevail — to find persons who feel such affinity for an unrelated child that they will repeatedly go out of

> "Paid child-rearing is rarely more than a weak stand-in for parental care. Someone is being asked to do for money what very few of us are able to do for any reason other than love."
>
> — Karl Zinsmeister

their way to do the things that make children thrive rather than merely survive."

Yet economic forces and cultural pressures push women into the labor force, and indirectly push young children into organized day care. Drawn by visions of personal fulfillment, women enter careers that require a full-time commitment. As child psychologist Bryna Siegal observes, many women ask themselves, "What would I rather be doing at 8:30 a.m., watching Joan Lunden doing 'Good Morning America' or being out there in a glamorous job like Joan Lunden's — with someone else watching my kids?"

Economic pressures force women to work longer hours than they would prefer. Many employed mothers would like to work fewer hours or work at home, to devote more time to their families. Researchers at Cornell University who examined the preferences of 224 dual wage-earner couples with young children found that a majority of mothers said they would prefer to work fewer hours so that they could have more time with their children.

However, since most working mothers feel that they *must* work full time, they have no alternative but to seek child care arrangements for their children. Consequently, they are often forced to leave infants and small children in situations that are far from ideal.

What should be acknowledged, say advocates of this first choice, is that children's needs come first. Public policy ought to be designed to encourage the kind of care that only parents can give to young children.

EFFECTS OF DAY CARE

Clearly, the trend is toward more organized child care outside the home. Today, most young children with working parents are cared for by nonrelatives. Although center-based care is less common than home day care for those age 4 and younger it is the fastest-growing type of child care. In just the last two years for which data are available, the fraction of children age 4 or younger who were placed in day care centers increased by more than 50 percent.

Advocates of this choice are convinced that this trend should not be encouraged. As they point out, the day-care debate often ignores crucial questions: What effect does it have on young children? How will increasing use of paid day care affect their development? How much day care is too much? How young is too young?

Although some researchers and many advocates of full-time day care claim that it is harmless or even beneficial to children's development, proponents of this first choice are convinced that full-time group care is not in the best interest of young children.

Even under optimal conditions, day care centers impose fixed routines and the kind of standardization that is the key to efficient operation of facilities in which dozens of children — in some centers, hundreds of children — are enrolled. What is frequently missing is individual attention, the recognition that some 4-year-olds thrive in the kind of regimen that others cannot tolerate.

All too often, staff turnover is high, which adds to the stressfulness of the situation. One of the few longitudinal

THE DAY CARE EXPERIMENT: THE PERILS OF FULL-TIME CARE

For five years, William and Wendy Dreskin operated a nonprofit preschool and day care center — an experience that prompted them to write The Day Care Decision: What's Best for You and Your Child *(New York: Evans, 1983). In this excerpt, they explain why they came to the conclusion that full-time alternative care of any kind is not in the best interest of children.*

In California, in 1973, we founded a nonprofit preschool for 3 to 5-year-olds because we were interested in early childhood development, and because we were idealistic about improving society. After operating a successful half-day preschool program for three years, we were confident that at least some of our goals were being accomplished.

But more and more mothers were going back to work and could not take advantage of a morning preschool. As rent and other expenses went up, it became increasingly difficult to make ends meet with the facility in use only three hours a day. We decided to open the school for full-time day care for 3 to 5-year-olds, and before- and after-school care for children in kindergarten through third grade.

We saw the clientele change from parents who cared about their children's educational development to parents who wanted a custodial arrangement.

Harried parents who wanted day care were rarely interested in seeing the brochure that described the program, and seldom asked to observe at the center. They simply asked the hours and the cost before enrolling. Very few seemed to be aware of how full-time care would affect the child's life.

For two years, we watched day care children in our day care center respond to the stresses of eight to ten hours a day of separation from their parents with tears, anger, withdrawal, or profound sadness. We found, to our dismay, that nothing in our own affection and caring for these children would erase this sense of loss and abandonment.

We saw some of the same boys and girls we had known as preschoolers (children who attended the program from 9:00 a.m. to noon) become different children when subjected to the stress of full-time day care. We came to realize that the *amount* of separation — the number of hours a day spent away from the parents — is a critical factor.

When parents become aware that their children are unhappy in day care, they usually assume that it is the fault of the particular sitter, the day care home, or the day care center. But very often the child is complaining about the lengthy daily separation from the parent, not about the condition of the toys or the careless attitude of day care workers. The result is that the message that day care itself causes the problem rarely gets through.

It took some time for us to realize that the children were often unhappy and missed their parents *despite* our doing a good job of meeting their individual needs and keeping them actively involved in projects and activities throughout the long day.

After a year and a half, we could no longer bear to watch. It was obvious that the children did not feel that staff understanding and comforting were adequate compensation for spending 40 or 50 hours a week away from their parents. There is a problem inherent in day care itself, a problem that hangs like a dark storm over "good" and "bad" day care centers alike. The children are too young to spend so much time away from their parents.

Out of a sense of obligation to the unhappy day care children at our center, we found ourselves talking the center out of business. When parents inquired about the program, we told them to try if possible to work part time until the children were older. Finally, when we realized that we could not in good conscience continue to be day care providers — no matter how much people clamored about the need for day care in the community — we decided to close the center.

Parents are beginning to question the day care experiment, a system in which young children spend most of their waking hours away from the family. They are also questioning the assumption that this is the Way of the Future. We felt an obligation to the unhappy day care children at our center, and to all children in day care, to explain why — with the best intentions — day care facilities can't "replace" children's parents on a daily basis.

> ## "After more than 30 years of research on how children develop, I would not think of putting an infant or toddler of my own into a center-based program."
> — Burton White

studies of the effects of day care — a study that followed the same children over time to observe long-term effects — was conducted in Britain by Terrence Moore, who showed that a succession of care givers is bad for children. By contrast, said Moore, "where a mother keeps her children in her own care full time to the age of five, the child tends early to internalize adult standards of behavior, notably self-control and intellectual achievement."

Studies by child development specialists suggest that extensive nonparental care early in life can lead to increased insecurity, misbehavior, aggressiveness, and withdrawal. The latest findings come as no surprise to anyone familiar with studies of child development that have been accumulating for decades. In 1974, for example, the federal government's Office of Child Care Development & Programs published a handbook for day care professionals that contained this passage: "Any responsible person involved with day care must recognize the danger it may hold for children and families. Enthusiasm for the potential benefits should be tempered by the realization that day care can be a source of harm."

A recent study conducted by University of Texas researchers Deborah Lowe Vandell and Mary Anne Corasanti helped to identify the effects of early separation. They found that children who are in day care from an early age are more likely to be uncooperative and unpopular by the third grade. The researchers also found that full-time day care is associated with poorer study skills, lower grades, and diminished self-esteem. Even children who entered full-time day care after their first year did not develop as well socially, emotionally, or intellectually as children in part-

SURELY YOU DON'T EXPECT _ME_ TO TAKE CARE OF MY OWN BABIES, DO YOU?

PHILA. DEPT. of HUMAN SERVICES FULL

SIGNE WILKINSON, *THE PHILADELPHIA DAILY NEWS*

time care or those whose mothers stayed home to care for them.

Obviously, factors such as the child's temperament and the relationship a child establishes with its parents have a lot to do with the adjustment to day care. The nature and quality of the program make a difference too. Still, advocates of this first choice conclude that a substantial amount of nonparental care — no matter how good that care is — poses a serious risk for young children.

Leading child development experts reach the same conclusion. Burton White, former director of the Harvard Preschool Project and author of *The First Three Years of Life*, says that "after more than 30 years of research on how children develop, I would not think of putting an infant or toddler of my own into a substitute care program

on a full-time basis, especially a center-based program." White advises parents that "unless you have a very good reason, I urge you not to delegate the primary child-rearing task to anyone else during your baby's first three years of life. . . . Babies form their first human attachment only once."

INFANTS AT RISK

Particularly worrisome to proponents of this position is the tendency to turn young children over to surrogate caretakers at an increasingly early age. Just a few decades ago, many school systems did not provide any formal schooling until age 6. Today, most communities offer kindergarten for 5-year-olds, and there is widespread experimentation with prekindergarten programs for 4-year-olds.

The next step was for day care centers to accept toddlers who are old enough to walk and feed themselves but need services such as diaper-changing that were formerly not provided by centers.

Most recently, and most disturbingly from this perspective, day care centers started to accommodate infants by redesigning their facilities to allow for cribs, high chairs, and bottle feeding. Once day care centers were equipped in this way, the age of children left in day care dropped to the six- or twelve-week-age limit imposed by most states.

The fact that about a third of the mothers of children under the age of one are employed full time in the labor force has sharply increased the demand for such facilities. Proponents of this choice feel strongly that nonmaternal care for infants is ill advised for several reasons.

In the first place, all forms of group care significantly increase the health risk. The home environment serves as a natural quarantine for infants and young children. But infant-toddler centers pose a substantial risk. In the words of Dr. Stephen Hadler, an epidemiologist with the Centers for Disease Control (CDC), "Day care centers are a fertile environment for the spread of infectious diseases, especially intestinally transmitted disease."

Infants and toddlers are at risk in group settings because they frequently put their hands and other objects in their mouths. Also, children who are not yet toilet trained increase the risk of infectious disease. For this reason, a pediatric task force on day care convened by the CDC recommended against group care for children still wearing diapers.

Studies of the health hazards of day care show that infants and toddlers trade not only colds and other minor health hazards but also more serious disease. The major illnesses associated with group care for children under two years are intestinally transmitted diseases like Hepatitis A and infections of the digestive tract, as well as infections of the respiratory system such as meningitis and influenza.

If there is substantial evidence of the health risk of group care to very young children, there is also mounting evidence of the emotional risk. In September 1986, Jay Belsky, a developmental psychologist at Pennsylvania State University, published a widely noted article in which he expressed

---

> "There is sufficient evidence that we know enough now to regard infant day care, as we have it in this nation, as a risk factor."
> — Jay Belsky

---

concern over a "slow, steady trickle" of accumulating negative evidence about the effects of day care, especially for infants less than a year old.

On the basis of his own research and that of other child development experts, Belsky warned that the mother-child bond may be impaired — and children may be at risk for future psychological and behavioral difficulties — when as infants they are separated from their mothers for more than 20 hours a week.

Like most day care researchers, Belsky cautions that additional long-term studies are needed before we can identify with certainty the effects of group care on infants. But he con-cludes that enough is known *now* to justify genuine concern about the trend toward group care for a significant fraction of America's youngest children. "There is sufficient evidence that we know enough now to regard infant day care, as we have it in this nation, as a risk factor."

PRO-FAMILY POLICY

The underlying problem, however, is that financial pressures have pushed many mothers into the workplace, leaving them no alternative other than to seek child care arrangements. Meanwhile, cultural support for childbearing and child rearing has eroded, and the economic position of parents has been allowed to deteriorate relative to other groups.

Advocates of this choice note how different the current situation is from the way in which parenthood was regarded in the post-World War II period. The pro-family orientation of that era was encouraged by the mass media and by public policy.

In a deliberate effort to relieve the financial burden of families with children, the tax code was restructured in 1948 and the personal exemption was raised from $200 to $600. That act represented a strong endorsement of the importance of parenthood. Consequently, most families with three or more children paid hardly any federal taxes.

As cultural support for parenting has declined, so have public incentives. If the federal tax exemption for dependents had been adjusted over the years to retain its 1948 value, parents would be allowed more than $6,000 per year in tax benefits for each of their children. Instead, the 1989 tax laws permit a personal exemption of only $2,000 per child.

> "The one thing parents can and should ask of government is to get out of the way. The best child care measures are to lower rates of taxing and spending."
> — David Kelley

One reflection of the support offered to families, say proponents of this view, is the inclination of adults to bear children. A strong pro-family tax policy in the 1950s was one reason why fertility rates were so high at the time. Today, however, because there is far less support for families, fewer adults are willing to make the sacrifices required to bear children and care for them. In recent years, the fertility rate of American women has been at a historic low level of about 1.8 children per woman — roughly half of what it was in the 1950s.

Proponents of this view conclude that we should reemphasize family roles and responsibilities. In the words of Allan C. Carlson, a commentator on family policy: "That task can only be achieved through a revitalized, family-affirming culture. We need normative arrangements that reinforce Americans who make a commitment to children and home. Except at the margin, these are clearly not tasks of government. A familial culture will either emerge out of the popular sentiments of the people, or it will not appear at all."

Proponents of this choice feel that the solution is *not* for government to provide more incentives for parents to place their children in day care facilities, which would encourage a trend that has already gone too far. According to a recent Labor Department report, the federal government currently spends $7 billion per year on child care, including Head Start, various block grants to the state, and child care tax credits. The recently enacted welfare reform program will boost that total when welfare recipients who take jobs start receiving child care support. There is no reason for government to spend more on child care. In the words of *Wall Street*

Journal columnist David Kelley: "The one thing parents can and should ask of government is to get out of the way. The best child care measures are to lower rates of taxing and spending."

Besides, direct government involvement in child care undermines the family by encouraging the notion that families are not responsible for the physical, financial, and emotional support of their own members. In this respect, the experience of welfare states such as Sweden is instructive. "The steady enlargement of child care responsibilities assumed by the Swedish state has led," says social critic George Gilder, "to an ever more rapid repudiation of child care responsibilities by families — to the point that more than 50 percent of Swedish children are born out of wedlock."

WHAT GOVERNMENT SHOULD DO

What, then, *should* be done? To reverse the trend toward reliance on child care provided outside the home, proponents of this view feel that government should make it easier for mothers to work for wages at home by changing regulations that currently inhibit home-based work. Also, work arrangements such as flex-time and shared-job options should be encouraged to permit parents to spend more time with their children.

Most of all, proponents of a pro-family solution insist that the most efficient way to encourage better child care is to change the tax codes. The Child Care Credit that discriminates against full-time mothers should be modified. Currently, the child care credit provides tax benefits only if the mother is in the labor force and pays for day care. But women who are full-time mothers are denied this benefit.

In this way, say advocates of this first choice, employed mothers are rewarded for *not* taking care of their own children. Moreover, the government penalizes families in which the mother stays at home by taxing them to cover the cost of subsidies for mothers who use day care.

People who share this perspective insist that government policy should encourage parental care of small children, not penalize it. In this respect, the United States should follow the example of France and West Germany, which provide mothers' allowances for this purpose.

Tax credits should go to *all* parents, not just to families that use organized day care. Child rearing should be regarded, in Allan Carlson's words, "as a vital service provided by families to society as a whole. Because the bearing and rearing of children is of tremendous importance to society, it is reasonable to expect that government should help couples who are raising children."

Providing more generous tax credits to all families with young children is the best way to help because it lets parents decide how to enhance the child's welfare, rather than forcing them to pay for "eligible providers" to qualify for public subsidies.

Endorsing the proposal to raise the tax exemption for children and to make a child care tax credit available to day care users and stay-at-home parents alike, Karl Zinsmeister writes that it would shift "a small portion of the burden for the care of young children onto the rest of society's shoulders. The tax burden lifted off child-raising families would be transferred to businesses, individuals, and households without family responsibilities. The improvements in family functioning and child welfare that should result would benefit the entire country."

WHAT CRITICS SAY

Critics of this choice admit that it would undoubtedly be good for children if their mothers stayed home to care for them. "It may be true that the best arrangement for most, if not all, young children is to live in a loving and safe environment with one or two siblings and their parents — according to the traditional pattern of a mother who stays at home, supported by an extended family and neighbors and a father who works," write child care experts Richard Ruopp and Jeffrey Travers. "But this is not the life a majority of parents are able to lead. What might be best for children cannot become the enemy of what can realistically be good for children."

As Representative James Florio put it in congressional hearings on child care held in February 1988, "nostalgia as public policy makes no sense." The majority of mothers of young children are wage earners today, and many of them work full time. Indeed, the standard of living of millions of American families increasingly depends upon their paycheck.

Besides, as critics of this first choice point out, stay-at-home mothers are not necessarily patient, loving caretakers of their children, contented in their role. Even when mothers make a conscious choice to stay home and care for their children, it is not always the best arrangement. Some women who forsake their careers to be full-time mothers feel trapped and unhappy. In such circumstances, the arrangement is neither in the mother's best interest nor in the child's.

With regard to the research conducted by child development experts and its relevance to the day care debate, critics of this first choice point out that the evidence is equivocal and does not support alarmist conclusions. Some child development experts point out the benefits of early group care, such as the knowledge and self-confidence young children gain from the experience.

In answer to concern about group care for very young children, psychologist Sandra Scarr plays down the significance of the care infants receive in their first year. "The emotional, social, and intellectual development of children in the first year of life is so protected by biological design that it's hard to get it off course in any permanent way by anything but abusive or neglectful environments."

Responding to public concern about the implications of recent studies on the impact of day care for young children, a group of child development experts led by Edward Zigler released a statement in 1988 supporting day care for infants and toddlers, while urging better salaries and training for day care workers. "There is every reason to believe," in the words of that statement, "that both children and families can thrive when parents have access to stable child-care arrangements featuring skilled, sensitive, and motivated care givers."

PUBLIC INITIATIVES

Many people are also critical of the policies proposed by advocates of this first choice. If tax credits were offered to families with young children, critics point out, there is no assurance that the money would be used to help young children. Such a proposal, as critics see it, is an income subsidy, not a child care program.

Moreover, if tax credits were provided to all families with young children — to those with a stay-at-home spouse as well as families in which mothers are wage earners — many of the benefits would end up in the hands of Americans who don't need government support.

Critics do not necessarily disagree with the objective of reducing the tax burden of families with young children — at least families at modest income levels. However, they point out that tax credit proposals that have been put forward — such as the Bush proposal for a tax credit of $1,000 a year for low-income parents of young children — amount to very little. So small a tax credit does not provide sufficient assistance to allow most mothers to stay home with their preschool children, or even to work part time to spend more daytime hours with them.

What makes more sense, many people believe, is to directly subsidize child care programs for low-income families. This is the child care policy preferred by advocates of a second course of action, to which we now turn. ∎

CHOICE #2
SOCIAL INVESTMENTS: A HEAD START FOR THE DISADVANTAGED

"Government has a clear role in providing organized day care, but only for children who are at risk. For disadvantaged children, Head Start-type programs offer a vital service and a real opportunity."

My children are presently in a day care center, writes a California woman, the single parent of two pre-schoolers, in a letter presented as testimony in congressional hearings in February 1989, "but I am months behind in my payments. There's no Head Start program in my community. I have a job that will eventually let me support my family on my own. I don't want to quit my job and become dependent on welfare. But I need help. Where can I get assistance?"

The woman's dilemma is shared by millions of American parents. They are low-income single parents struggling to remain self-sufficient and to stay off welfare. Or they are two-parent families in which the second income keeps the family from falling below the poverty line.

Since quality day care costs more than poor families can afford, they resort to expedients. They leave their jobs and go on welfare so that they can take care of their children. Or, in order to work, they leave their children in inadequate and sometimes dangerous child care situations — with older siblings, or in overcrowded or un-stimulating substitute care.

Despite the Head Start program, which serves some 450,000 preschoolers — mostly 3- and 4-year-olds from poor families — and other government efforts to subsidize child care for low-income children, public preschool programs are inadequate to the demand. Only about one in six children from eligible families actually attends a Head Start program. Even fewer infants and toddlers from poor families have access to high-quality child care programs, such as well-supervised family day care.

Proponents of this second choice regard the lack of affordable child care facilities for poor children as a serious

SUSIE FITZHUGH

problem, which should be remedied as our first order of public business. It has traditionally been the government's responsibility to respond to children in distress, whether they are abandoned, abused, or neglected. Today, the number of poor children at risk — preschoolers who are ill prepared to enter kindergarten and keep up with their more advantaged peers — is growing. Yet public subsidies for this purpose have lagged far behind the need.

Over the past two decades, even after accounting for inflation, federal subsidies for child care doubled. But most of that increase came in the form of child care tax credits, which benefit middle-income rather than low-income families, since most poor families are mainly off the tax rolls. As child care experts Douglas Besharov and Paul Tramontozzi write, "In this era when programs for the disadvantaged are under the gun, it is wrong to funnel scarce federal dollars to middle-class families who need them less. Priority should be given to families in greatest need."

Judging by the number of preschoolers from affluent families who participate in organized preschool programs, whether or not their mothers work, it appears that many parents have decided that such programs are good for their children and that they provide a stimulating environment for early learning. But because poor parents are often unable to afford developmental day care and because the government does not provide it, children from low-income families are less than half as likely to attend preschool programs compared to their more advantaged peers. Advocates of this second choice believe that this situation is not only inequitable but shortsighted.

"The experience of a literate environment in a program for 3-year-olds may

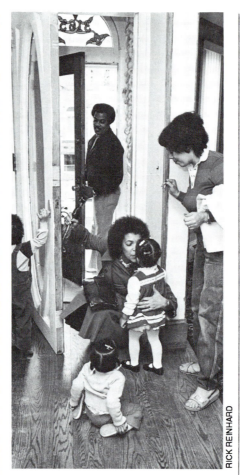

Saying goodbye: few low-income parents can afford quality day care.

be a pleasant icing on a happy middle-class childhood," comments Fred Hechinger, education columnist for the *New York Times*. "But for millions of poor children, many of whom are otherwise doomed to lifelong failure, a better start can be a social, economic, and intellectual lifesaver. For them, an early opportunity to take part in a verbal, literate, caring way of life, for at least part of the day, is no frill. It could be the crucial chance to introduce them into the mainstream of American life."

Proponents of this view insist that if parents can afford only a fraction of the cost of quality care for preschoolers, it

is not in the child's best interest — nor is it in the public interest — for them to be consigned to substandard care.

HEAD START

Project Head Start, which was launched in 1965 as part of the War on Poverty, was the first major government-financed effort to meet the needs of poor children before they enter kindergarten. It was designed to prepare disadvantaged children for traditional schooling, and to help children and their families achieve economic self-sufficiency.

By the mid-1960s, it was evident to many people that poor children need special help if they are expected to compete on an equal basis with their more fortunate peers. The work of educational psychologist Benjamin Bloom was influential in showing that slow development in a child's early years may be irremediable. In his book *Stability and Change in Human Characteristics*, Bloom argued that the long-term effects of living in a culturally deprived environment frequently lower a child's measured intelligence by as much as twenty points. A deficit of that size describes the difference between a youngster considered barely educable, unfit even for many kinds of unskilled work, and one who might succeed in college.

In the words of educator Douglas Carnine, "Most 5-year-olds from low-income backgrounds enter school with far fewer skills and concepts than their more advantaged peers." The chief purpose of Head Start is to provide an explicitly educational early childhood program that gives disadvantaged children an equal opportunity when they enter public school.

Head Start was spurred by another motive, the recognition of the severity of poverty for millions of families. If

> ## "Most 5-year-olds from low-income backgrounds enter school with far fewer skills and concepts than their more advantaged peers."
> ### — Douglas Carnine

poor families — particularly single-parent and adolescent mothers — are to become economically independent, parents must have access to affordable, high-quality, full-day child care.

From the beginning, Head Start was intended as a comprehensive child development program that serves the whole child. While the program emphasizes the development of conceptual and verbal skills, it provides other services. It enhances young children's physical health, promotes their emotional and social development, and builds a sense of self-worth. In various ways, the program emphasizes parental involvement.

Head Start, which began as a 6-week summer program, has been expanded over the years. In most communities, it now consists of a half-day program offered throughout the school year. It serves about 450,000 children between the ages of 3 and 5, mainly from families whose income is at or below the poverty line. The annual cost is slightly more than $1 billion — which amounts to an average per child cost of about $2,700.

Because it is generally regarded, as President Carter put it in 1980, as "a program that works," Head Start is praised by liberals and conservatives alike. A symbol of the nation's commitment to help poor children advance by their own efforts, it enjoys enthusiastic support both in local communities and on Capitol Hill.

WHAT HAPPENED IN YPSILANTI

As proponents of this choice see it, Head Start is an investment that pays off — for children, for families, for communities, and for the nation as a whole. Many of the claims about the benefits of preschool compensatory education are based upon a long-term study of Perry Preschool Program in Ypsilanti, Michigan. In the

THE AFFORDABILITY CRUNCH

According to the Census Bureau, while roughly a third of the parents who choose child care use unpaid care, generally provided by relatives, most parents pay for it. The cost of child care varies widely. Family day care, for example, costs less on average than day care centers. On an annual basis, the average cost of care per child is approximately $3,000.

Whether the household has one wage earner or two, millions of families — especially poor families who are already spending a large fraction of their income on housing, food, and other necessities — cannot afford to pay for decent child care.

Young parents beginning their working lives often have low wages. In 1988, the total household income of 7.1 million American families fell below the poverty line of $9,100 for a family of 3. For these families, the cost of child care is prohibitive.

For single-parent families — in which one in five American children is now raised — the problem of affording child care is particularly acute. The median annual income for a single mother with at least one child younger than 6 was only $7,013 in 1988. Costs of child care for one child equal nearly half of what a person working full time at minimum wage earns.

PERCENTAGE OF INCOME THAT LOW-INCOME PARENTS WOULD HAVE TO PAY FOR CHILD CARE

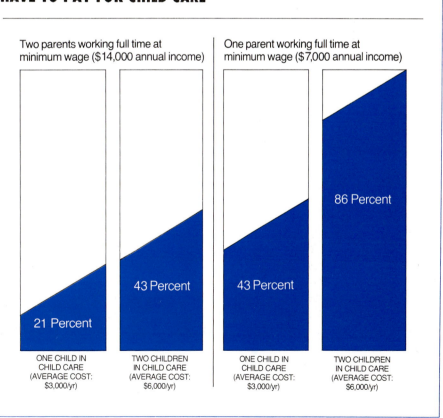

Two parents working full time at minimum wage ($14,000 annual income)

One parent working full time at minimum wage ($7,000 annual income)

21 Percent — ONE CHILD IN CHILD CARE (AVERAGE COST: $3,000/yr)

43 Percent — TWO CHILDREN IN CHILD CARE (AVERAGE COST: $6,000/yr)

43 Percent — ONE CHILD IN CHILD CARE (AVERAGE COST: $3,000/yr)

86 Percent — TWO CHILDREN IN CHILD CARE (AVERAGE COST: $6,000/yr)

"PILE OF BLOCKS?..... I WAS THINKING OF IT AS A LONG OVERDUE FIRST STEP TOWARD TRAINING THE LEADERS OF TOMORROW, INTO WHOSE HANDS WILL FALL THE AWESOME TASK OF RESTORING AMERICA'S FALTERING GLOBAL COMPETITIVENESS."

JOEL PETT, LEXINGTON HERALD-LEADER

1960s, researchers began tracking students who attended the program to see what difference it made in the lives of impoverished children.

In 1984, a report on the long-term effects of that program entitled *Changed Lives* was released. It was a longitudinal study that compared 58 students who attended the preschool program in Ypsilanti at ages 3 and 4 with 65 other poor children from the same community who did not attend preschool.

The study provides striking evidence of the effectiveness of intensive preschool programs. By the time graduates of the Perry Preschool reached their late teens, they fared much better than children who did not attend preschool. They were far less likely to fail in school or to fall behind grade level. The high school graduation rate for Perry Preschool graduates was almost one-third higher, and they were more likely to attend college. Moreover, they were arrested less often and less likely to become juvenile delinquents. Compared to

their non-preschool counterparts, they were far less likely as young adults to become dependent upon welfare assistance.

That report on the long-term effects of the Perry Preschool Program established what advocates of compensatory preschool programs had long believed. Quality preschool programs improve the life chances of poor children. They reduce dropout rates. And they increase the likelihood of eventually becoming employed and economically self-sufficient.

While other studies of the effect of Head Start programs have typically shown somewhat more modest gains, they too have demonstrated the advantages of preschool programs, especially for poor black children. In the words of Ron Haskins, an expert on child development who serves as a staff member to the House Committee on Ways and Means, "The studies demonstrate unequivocally that quality preschool programs can provide an

immediate boost to children's intellectual performance and reduce their rate of placement in special education classes. The studies also provide evidence that quality preschool programs increase the likelihood of high school graduation."

However, even Head Start's staunch advocates warn that it is not an inoculation that guarantees long-term educational success. Countering the effects of poverty has to be a continuous process.

Still, Head Start accomplishes what it promised. Proponents of this choice conclude that an expanded day care program for poor children represents a sound social investment because it helps to break the cycle of poverty. It enables single, poor mothers in particular to get off welfare and to become productive workers. And it allows poor children to perform on a more equal basis with their more advantaged peers when they start school together.

POOR KIDS

The problem, from this perspective, is that despite the proven success of Head Start, it reaches relatively few of those who could benefit from it. The 450,000 preschoolers currently enrolled in Head Start programs represent only about 16 percent of those who are eligible. Over 1,000 counties throughout the nation still do not participate in Head Start.

Even where Head Start programs are available, they are generally part-time programs. While most parents work 40-50 hours a week and at least 50 weeks a year, in most communities Head Start is a half-day program, offered during the 34 weeks of a school year. Consequently, parents have to pay for additional arrangements for the care of their preschool-

> "Quality preschool programs improve the life chances of poor children. They reduce dropout rates, and they increase the likelihood of eventually becoming employed and self-sufficient."

ers when Head Start is not in session.

Most serious, from this perspective, is the fact that while the number of slots in Head Start facilities has remained about the same in recent years, the number of preschoolers who need publicly subsidized day care has grown.

Contrary to the widespread belief that the poor constitute only a small minority, more than 5 million children under the age of 6 live in poverty. "We have become a society," writes Senator Daniel Patrick Moynihan, "divided into two kinds of families. In this dual-family system, many of our children, randomly but inexorably, are born without a fair chance."

The statistics provide a sobering profile of poverty among America's youngest citizens. About one in four preschoolers comes from a poor family. Poverty is especially common among black and Hispanic children. Thirty-eight percent of all Hispanic children are poor. Among blacks, 43 percent are poor.

In most poor families, at least one parent works. But since a full-time, year-round job at the minimum wage yields only 72 percent of the federal poverty level for a family of three, such families need another wage earner. Consequently, in two-parent families, women are obliged to work.

Maintaining an adequate family income is a particular problem for the growing number of single-parent families. Among children born into single-parent households, one in two is poor. The increasing number of such families — which in most cases are headed by a woman — is one of the startling social developments of the last few decades, and it is one of the chief reasons why demand for day care among low-income families has risen.

In 1965, when Head Start went into effect, only 7 percent of white children

and 24 percent of black children lived in one-parent families. By 1988, those percentages more than doubled: 19 percent of white children and 54 percent of black children now live in one-parent households. Because women who raise children alone frequently have no income other than their own earnings, and because their wages are often quite modest, they are particularly vulnerable.

Considering the number of families that are poor despite their work effort, proponents of this choice conclude that there is a growing need for public day care. For poor families, some of whom are obliged to spend 20 percent or more of their family income for this purpose, day care is an unbearable financial burden.

In many instances, the absence of reliable child care arrangements is one of the chief reasons why unemployed mothers do not work. In 1985, the Roper Organization asked women whether the lack of child care keeps them from working outside the home. Among women in households earning less than $15,000 annually, two-thirds said they certainly would take advantage of day care to seek employment for themselves.

To proponents of this choice, these are compelling arguments for providing day care to all children from poor families. In the words of a report from the High/Scope Educational Research Foundation: "Without more help than they now get, impoverished children are likely to grow up without a chance as adults to make productive contributions to society." Instead, they are likely to be costly liabilities to society. Their mothers, in many instances, will be forced to remain at home, dependent on welfare.

SOCIAL INVESTMENT

While there has been growing recognition — particularly at the state level — of the need to expand child care services for the poor, what is currently done falls far short of the needs of families and children. As the situation of children in poor families has deteriorated, federal assistance for such families has declined.

Critics of recent government initiatives point to the Title XX block grants, one of the chief ways in which the federal government assists poor

families with young children. In 1982, child care programs using Title XX money served only 14 percent of the 3.4 million children younger than 6 who lived in poverty. Two years later, almost 5 million children were in that situation, but Title XX funds had been reduced by a combination of budget cuts and inflation.

During the 1980s, as already noted, the only federal subsidies for child care that grew substantially — child care tax credits — mainly benefited middle-class families, not the families that most need help. A far more sensible approach to child care, say proponents of this choice, is to regard it as a social investment and to make it available to poor families who need it most.

Over the past few years, there has been growing awareness, as there was in the mid-1960s, of poverty and the long-term cost of ignoring the needs of the disadvantaged. A 1987 report from the Committee for Economic Development, entitled *Children in Need: Investment Strategies for the Educationally Disadvantaged*, warns of an emerging "permanent underclass of young people" who cannot hold jobs because they lack fundamental literacy skills and work habits.

The report, prepared by a group of corporate executives, stressed the economic implications of recent trends: "This nation cannot continue to compete and prosper in the global arena when more than one-fifth of our children live in poverty and a third grow up in ignorance. The nation can ill afford such an egregious waste of human resources."

In the words of one of the contributors to that report, Owen B. Butler, retired chairman of Procter and Gamble, "American business has learned over the last ten years that it is

FRANK MODELL, COPYRIGHT 1973 *THE NEW YORKER MAGAZINE, INC.*

> "We have become a society divided into two kinds of families. Many of our children, randomly but inexorably, are born without a fair chance."
>
> — Senator Daniel Patrick Moynihan

a lot more effective to design quality in from the beginning than to correct things later." Considering the current rates of illiteracy, unemployability, poverty, drug use, and despair among the disadvantaged, says Butler, it makes more sense to spend money now on early childhood intervention.

The same message is heard increasingly from elected officials, and not just those representing America's urban areas. In his State of the State address in 1989, Idaho Governor Cecil Andrus said, "We must help children at risk. Either we will help our children become responsible and self-sufficient, or we will pay, and pay dearly, to provide many of them with welfare or put many of them in jail."

FROM TALK TO ACTION

Advocates of this choice insist that we should move from talk to action by guaranteeing child care to parents who cannot afford to pay for it. Head Start, or a similar publicly funded program, should be provided to every 3- and 4-year-old child. The government should also provide vouchers or scholarships for day care centers or family care for infants and toddlers from low-income families.

Recognizing, in the words of National Education Association President Mary Futrell, that "one cannot overstate the importance of the early childhood years in relation to future success in school or in life." We ought to decide that providing full-time day care for the disadvantaged is a public obligation and a prudent social investment.

Proponents of day care for the disadvantaged regard the fact that various states are considering public programs for disadvantaged 4-year-olds as a step in the right direction. In Michigan, Governor James Blanchard has called for public preschool within three years for every at-risk 4-year-old.

SUSIE FITZHUGH

The problem, from this perspective, is that the proposals currently being discussed are not comprehensive enough. Several dozen states have proposed a half-day program for 4-year-olds. However, disadvantaged children and their parents need something more: a full-day, year-round program that accommodates the needs of 2- and 3-year-olds as well as 4-year-olds. Infants and children under 2 from poor families also need quality programs to prepare them for Head Start when they are three.

A comprehensive effort of this sort would be costly. But as proponents of this choice see it, this is not an area in which it makes sense to economize or to settle for token efforts. Spending $1 now for quality preschool saves at least several dollars later on in public expenses for remedial education, crime control, and welfare.

Since day care for the disadvantaged allows poor mothers to enter the labor force — to move from the welfare rolls into a situation where they are taxpaying citizens — the savings would start immediately. In the words of Marian Wright Edelman, president of the Chil-

dren's Defense Fund, Head Start should be regarded as a "welfare prevention" strategy. The broader it is, the more effective it is likely to be in this respect.

The experience of Head Start shows that quality preschool and compensatory education programs lower the dropout rate, and they help to produce better-prepared students and more trainable workers. Proponents of this view are convinced programs such as Head Start should be made available to all 3- and 4-year-olds from poor families. Furthermore, we should provide additional public assistance for the care of poor children under the age of 3.

Advocates of this second choice conclude that there is a clear role for government in providing day care — but only for children who are at risk. "The enthusiasm for child care subsidies for most families with young children," writes *Newsweek* columnist Robert Samuelson, "obscures this reality: that they divert scarce funds from the truly needy. A compassionate government ought to concentrate its resources on its neediest — that is, poorest — citizens."

WHAT CRITICS SAY

While few people deny the importance of helping the disadvantaged, the proposal to expand Head Start substantially is criticized from several directions — and not just on the grounds that it would be very costly.

A second criticism comes from people concerned about accelerating family breakdown and encouraging higher birth rates among the disadvantaged. They say that social welfare programs for the poor tend to undermine the family, and contribute to the tendency toward single-parent households. Providing public day care for preschoolers may exacerbate the problem and encourage even more births among the women who are least able to raise children to be productive members of society.

The most frequently voiced criticism of this proposal raises questions about whether Head Start has been oversold, and whether it deserves to be greatly expanded. Repeatedly, media accounts convey the message that preschool programs for poor children have been proved effective, that in the long run the benefits more than repay the public's investment.

"Year after year," write Enid Borden and Kate Walsh O'Beirne, former federal social service officials, "Democrats and Republicans alike tout Head Start as a program that works and one that should be greatly expanded. Compensatory preschool education for poor children is clearly good politics, but is it good policy?"

Like other critics of Head Start, Borden and O'Beirne conclude that

President Bush at a Head Start center.

many of the claims for Head Start are exaggerated. In particular, they warn against generalizing from the results of the Perry Preschool Program. The reason it produced such striking results was that it operated under ideal circumstances. The program had an ample budget and an unusually capable and dedicated staff. Teachers visited each student's home for more than an hour each week while the program was in session. It was, in brief, a model program, a recipe for success. But it was hardly typical. For this reason, it is foolish to assume that most preschool programs yield the same striking results.

Not surprisingly, studies of other Head Start programs have shown more modest effects. None, for example, has demonstrated such dramatic reductions in teen pregnancy, crime, and welfare dependency.

Significantly, while most studies have shown immediate gains in academic performance, by the end of the second year of elementary school there is no discernible difference between children who attended Head Start programs and those who did not.

"In short," writes Ron Haskins, "the literature on preschool education does not support the claim that a program of national scope would yield lasting impacts on children's school performance nor substantial returns on the investment of public dollars."

Few people disagree about the importance of trying to assist poor youngsters, or searching for an effective welfare prevention strategy. "But we cannot afford to pretend," write Enid Borden and Kate Walsh O'Beirne, "that Head Start breaks this cycle. The weight of evidence does not support the idea that enrolling one million more children in the program as currently structured will improve their educational prospects."

Even some supporters of developmental day care for the disadvantaged are not comfortable with the proposal to expand Head Start-type programs. The problem with this solution, they say, is that it creates a poor children's "track," which is undesirable on educational as well as social grounds.

Moreover, until child care is provided to preschoolers at *all* income levels, it won't have much political support. For this reason, the expansion of Head Start is likely to be sidetracked, and the program itself is likely to be perennially underfunded. It will never get the resources it needs. In any case, as some people see it, there are compelling reasons why families at *all* income levels should be guaranteed high-quality day care — which is the premise of our third choice.■

CHOICE #3
A PUBLIC COMMITMENT: UNIVERSAL DAY CARE

"The care of preschoolers is a public problem that requires a clearly defined government role. All families with young children should have access to affordable, high-quality day care."

Of all the changes in American life over the past generation, none is so striking as the alterations in women's roles. Advertisements, magazine articles, and TV shows feature women who juggle their work, their marriages, and their child care responsibilities. The working mother, holding her briefcase in one hand and her child in the other, is one of the icons of the 1980s. Tales of harried mothers whose lives are thrown into disarray when child care arrangements break down are a sign of the times.

A *New York Times* article about the complications of modern family life featured the experience of a 34-year-old consumer research manager for Procter and Gamble, a married woman whose support network broke down. "Every day after dropping off her two preschool children at the baby-sitter's, Carol Berning went to work with a knot in her stomach. She found herself staring at her youngsters' pictures and worrying. The sitter had been letting them play in the street, and worse, she was taking them on unscheduled trips. Then, unexpectedly, the sitter resigned and the chore of finding a replacement soon absorbed much of Mrs. Berning's workday."

Most parents could tell the same story from their own experience. At all income levels, parents have a hard time juggling work and family respon-

BRIAN DUFFY, *THE DES MOINES REGISTER*

sibilities. Even the most elaborate child care arrangements tend to fall apart.

Family life has changed decisively, not only for low-income families but for *most* Americans. The transition to a situation in which most mothers of young children maintain wage-paying jobs has been dramatically swift. Yet the institutions parents depend upon for support — particularly the workplace and the schools — have not yet adapted to new realities. While the number of employers offering some form of child care assistance has risen from 50 in 1970 to more than 3,000, such benefits are available to only about 1 employee in 100.

Most Western European nations have long since recognized that the care of preschool children is a legitimate public concern. France, for example, has a well-developed system of centers that provide high-quality child care, largely at public expense. In most nations, it is understood that children are a valuable national resource, and that parents need child care in order to work. But in the United States, the care of preschool children remains mainly a private responsibility. Parents are expected to do the job on their own.

This is the point of departure for our third choice, which insists that pre-school programs for children from families at all income levels should become a public responsibility. This should happen, say proponents of this third choice, for the same reason that grammar school was first provided at public expense a century ago, for the same reason that Social Security became a public program half a century ago. The care of preschoolers is a *public* problem, which deserves a comprehensive solution and requires a clearly defined government role.

"Because of changes that have taken place in the American family," write child care experts Edward Zigler and Jody Goodman, "day care is no longer simply a service that enables poor women to work. It has become an essential part of a much broader national picture. Day care is not just for children. It's for working mothers. It's for fathers, so their wives can help support the family. It's for families, so children can grow up in a healthy environment. And it's for people who don't have children, so the economy can run smoothly."

The argument for a public commitment to universal child care rests on five assertions:
- Because of new economic realities, most mothers *must* work to augment family income.
- Despite the demand for child care, existing facilities are woefully inadequate. Consequently, many preschoolers are deprived of what they could benefit from: quality, developmental day care.
- Because the day care system is a patchwork, families at all income levels feel stress caused by juggling work and family obligations.
- Because the current situation is particularly stressful for women, it is an impediment to their equal participation in the labor force.
- To compete successfully in the world economy, America should encourage women's participation in the labor force. One of the best ways to do so is to offer comprehensive, high-quality day care to children from all types of families.

Let us examine these five assertions and the prescription for public action to which they lead.

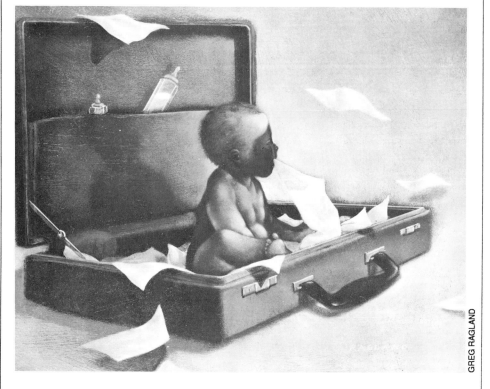

GREG RAGLAND

ECONOMIC NECESSITY

The argument for universal day care begins with the assertion that mothers in most American families are obliged to work in order to augment family income. Average weekly wages, adjusted for inflation, have declined by about 15 percent since 1973. Over that period, the average annual earnings of men in their twenties declined by almost 30 percent.

In many cases, the woman's paycheck — which amounts on average to 20 to 30 percent of family income — keeps her family's income above the poverty line. If families had to do without women's wages, it is estimated that the poverty rate would go up by at least a third. Increasingly, child care is necessary to permit mothers to continue working, so that their families remain economically self-sufficient.

This is a significant change from the situation of the post-World War II era, when a single income was in most cases sufficient to maintain a middle-class life-style, and when most women left the labor force soon after they married to bear and rear children.

Today, some 70 percent of women currently in the work force are in their childbearing years. Eighty percent of these women are expected to bear children at some point during the course of their employment. With only a brief time-out for childbirth and the care of newborns, most mothers return to the workplace, where they are expected to perform their jobs while caring for young children.

Proponents of this view are convinced that maternal employment — and the temporary separation it causes between mothers and their children — is not harmful to preschoolers. As Kamerman and Hayes conclude in

"Mommy will see you later. Mommy has to go to law school now."

ROBERT WEBER, COPYRIGHT 1982 *THE NEW YORKER MAGAZINE*, INC.

their book *Families That Work*, research shows that *if* the mother wants to work, *if* the child care is of reasonable quality, and *if* the family is not unusually stressed, there is no reason for concern about adverse effects on young children.

What should concern us, say people who approach the child care issue from this perspective, is that many of the children whose mothers work in full-time jobs are left in situations that are far from satisfactory.

A PATCHWORK SYSTEM

Advocates of this choice insist that high-quality day care is good for young children. It stimulates their intellectual development and facilitates the development of social skills. Yet in many communities, good child care is either unavailable or unaffordable. When facilities are available, they are often second-rate programs, run by underpaid staff.

"Across the country," says Marian Wright Edelman, "we hear reports about an increasingly vulnerable child care system which threatens the safety and well-being of our children. Too many facilities are considering closing their doors because they can no longer retain staff. Too many parents have no idea where to turn in their communities to locate decent child care."

Private nursery schools, family day care, and nationally franchised day care centers have all expanded. But the supply of affordable, high-quality child care facilities falls far short of the demand. Across the country, parents report problems in locating satisfactory child care facilities. In a study of employees with young children in New Jersey companies, almost half of the respondents said that locating high-quality child care is a major problem.

CHARACTERISTICS OF HIGH-QUALITY CARE

Many proponents of an expanded government role in child care are at least as concerned about the *quality* of such facilities as they are about providing a sufficient number of child care "slots." In the words of Owen B. Butler, "the alarming talk about child care 'slots' makes them sound like parking spaces for children. We should be asking not just how to provide the 'slots' but what happens to children in the child care settings we provide."

A critical question, from this perspective, is what standard government should insist on. Currently, although all states regulate day care centers and most regulate family day care as well, the requirements of child care providers as well as the level of enforcement vary widely. While standards in some states are consistent with generally accepted definitions of quality care, other states fail to insist upon anything more than minimal levels of health and safety. Consequently, some preschoolers are indeed "parked" in inadequate facilities.

What constitutes quality care for preschoolers? As the Department of Health and Human Services noted in a 1985 report, "no single set of standards can be applied practically to all the unique child care situations." Still, child care experts agree upon certain general guidelines. When examining child care facilities, writes Bettye M. Caldwell, professor of Education at the University of Arkansas at Little Rock, parents should ask a series of questions. Advocates of this third choice conclude that the states should insist upon the following standards for all child care providers.

- Do you see a license indicating that the facility meets state standards or has accreditation from the National Association for the Education of Young Children?

- Are enough adults available to care adequately for the children? Here are reasonable ratios:
    Infants: At least one adult for every four babies
    Toddlers: At least one adult for every six to eight children
    Preschoolers: At least one adult for every ten to twelve children
    Five-year-olds: At least one adult for every twelve to fifteen children

- Are staff members trained in child development and early childhood education, and in procedures necessary for maintaining healthful conditions in group programs?

CATHY BLAIVAS

- Are there medical prerequisites (thorough examination, immunization) for enrollment, specified procedures to be followed in emergencies, and carefully kept records on both children and the staff?

- Are rigorous sanitary procedures followed by the staff (such as careful hand washing after every diaper change and prior to any food handling) which will minimize the spread of infections among the children?

- Does the center have an acceptable place for the care of children who become ill during the day?

- Is the facility securely fenced, and is there a safe place for delivering and picking up children?

- Does the place look and smell fresh and clean?

- Is there a planned daily program that helps children develop emotionally, socially, and intellectually?

- Does the center's philosophy of discipline show respect for children and promote self-esteem?

- Do the children spend most of their time in fairly small groups (specifically, no more than eight to ten babies, twelve to fifteen preschoolers)?

- Do there seem to be enough toys, books, and playground equipment for the number of children enrolled?

- Is adequate space and time set aside for naps and rest?

- Are field trips carefully planned and supervised? Are parents invited to accompany the groups on excursions?

- Are parents free to visit at any time and encouraged to remain with their children during the first several days after enrollment?

- Are you offered a booklet providing details of such things as fees, your responsibilities and privileges, and those of the center?

> "Child care workers are paid less per hour than animal caretakers, bartenders, and parking lot attendants. It is not surprising that so many move on to other kinds of work."

The problem is particularly acute among families with infants and toddlers. When family day care is available for very young children, its quality is often uncertain. Though facilities for the daytime care of children younger than two have expanded, rapidly escalating demand for such care, coupled with its high cost, makes the task of finding and paying for such care especially difficult. In one city after another, facilities offering such services report long waiting lists.

Furthermore, say proponents of this third choice, cost is a problem. Even dual wage-earner middle-class families often have trouble finding facilities they can afford. The cost of full-time day care averages about $3,000 per year per child, and infant care costs even more. Especially in families with two or more preschoolers, that is a hefty expense. After shelter, food, and taxes, it is a working family's biggest expense. In all too many cases, financial pressures force parents to resort to less expensive, and less than satisfactory, arrangements.

In the absence of consistent standards for child care facilities, quality is uneven. Currently, the federal government sets no standards for child care programs, even those receiving federal funds. State child care regulations do not guarantee quality, and they are often unenforced. For example, while group size may affect how much children learn — as well as their health and safety — 31 states fail to regulate group size for preschoolers, and 25 states do not regulate size for infant care centers. Some states have no specific health training requirements for staff in child care centers. And many do nothing to guarantee parents' rights to visit child care programs at any time to assess the quality and safety of the program.

In Minneapolis, a privately run facility called Chicken Soup caters to the needs of children who are too sick to attend regular child care programs.

"In the United States," said psychologist Deborah Phillips, testifying in 1988 to a Senate Subcommittee, "the federal government regulates meat, highway speed limits, airline safety, and most financial institutions. We eliminate dangerous drugs, contaminated food, and building insulation that doesn't meet health standards — and for good reason." Is it unreasonable, she asks, "to hold child care centers and family day care homes to a uniform floor of quality below which the health, safety, and development of children are likely to be jeopardized?"

Critics of current day care arrangements are also concerned about how little child care workers are paid — and about the high staff turnover that results. Because child care in the United States is a cottage industry, the individuals who provide such care are not regarded as professionals, nor are they paid equivalent wages. According to the Census Bureau, elementary school teachers earned an average of $422 per week in 1987, and their turnover rate per year was 9 percent. Child care workers, however, earned less than half that amount — $182 per week, and each year 42 percent of them leave day care for other kinds of work. Only half of them receive health benefits and fewer than one in five has a retirement plan.

Overall, child care workers are paid less per hour and receive fewer benefits than animal caretakers, bartenders, and parking lot attendants. It is not surprising, from this perspective, that many child care workers move on to other kinds of work.

Advocates of this view insist that the care of young children is vitally important. Its importance should be reflected in the priority we attach to providing a stimulating, nurturing environment for young children, as well as the salaries paid to dedicated and well-trained day care professionals.

FAMILIES IN DISTRESS

Without a comprehensive child care system, say advocates of this choice, it is difficult for parents to juggle work and family responsibilities. While working women with school-age children typically balance various demands and experience considerable satisfaction in doing so, studies of couples with preschoolers report high levels of stress and marital discord. A study of parents employed at Merck and Co., Inc., for example, found that more than two-thirds of the mothers of young children experienced high levels of work-family conflict.

As sociologist Kristina Cooper explains: "These couples must deal with the multiple role requirements of being a spouse, parent, and working person. When the children are very young, the parental role is especially demanding, taking time away from the spousal and work roles."

A growing body of research documents what most working parents already know — that because of fragile child care arrangements, parental productivity suffers, absenteeism increases, and workers are sometimes forced to quit because of a lack of adequate child care. In one recent study at a large corporation in the Boston area, researchers found that one-third of the employees — male and female — said they frequently worry about their children during the day. More than 40 percent said the strain of managing family responsibilities is the main reason they get depressed at work.

The same pattern has been demonstrated in other studies, such as a survey of more than 8,000 employed parents in Oregon, which found that roughly half the women and more than one-quarter of the men reported stress related to child care. Significantly, parents at all income levels reported roughly similar levels of stress.

Moreover, breakdowns in child care arrangements are a frequent occurrence. In research conducted at the Bank Street College in New York, Ellen Galinsky found that over the three months prior to the survey 63 percent of the employees had to make special arrangements at least once because their usual child care arrangements had broken down.

Considering the complexity of the child care arrangements to which many parents are forced to resort, breakdowns are not surprising. After studying child care arrangements, Alfred Kahn and Sheila Kamerman wrote, "We see desperate parents 'packaging' parts of a child's day in one facility, and parts of a day in another, or with a relative or neighbor. We see them moving their children two or

UPI/BETTMANN NEWSPHOTOS

three times a year because of dissatisfaction with care arrangements or the disappearance of care givers. We see them desperately going from one transportation and pick-up arrangement to another."

When child care arrangements break down, parents often have no alternative but to set aside work responsibilities to care for their children. A survey conducted by The Conference Board for *Fortune* magazine found that problems with child care arrangements are the single most common cause of absenteeism and unproductive work time. As indicated in a recent report from the Census Bureau, one in every 20 working parents is absent from work at least 1 day each month because of child care problems.

Clearly, the absence of reliable child care arrangements is a source of stress for parents of young children, and a factor that adversely affects job performance. We must build a child care system, conclude advocates of this choice, that allows working families the peace of mind they need to be productive on their jobs.

WOMEN'S WORK

One of the benefits of a universal system of preschool care, say proponents of this choice, is that it would reduce the tension between the demands of motherhood and the demands of the workplace, and thus permit women to participate in the labor force on an equal basis with men.

Although many mothers now work at full-time jobs outside the home, very little has changed regarding women's child-rearing responsibilities or housekeeping duties. Even when they are full-time wage earners, women typically perform most of the child-rearing duties such as making arrange-

> "We regard child care as the key that opens the door to women's equality."
> — Barbara McDougall

ments for daytime care, or staying home when children are sick. It is no surprise, then, that women are more often absent from work than their male peers. Studies show that women miss work for this reason twice as often as men.

Women's performance at work is also more likely to be affected by worries about child care. Since women are more directly responsible for the welfare of their children, they more often report feeling stress on the job caused by worries about child care.

Moreover, when husbands and wives get home at the end of the workday, women do more of the housekeeping and child care chores. While there is growing support among men for the view that both sexes *ought* to share responsibility for domestic chores in dual wage-earner families, what husbands say in this respect does not describe what they do.

This helps to explain why mothers — particularly mothers of young children — have more trouble keeping good jobs and advancing to positions that offer higher wages. Largely because of the competing claims of motherhood, there are important differences between the careers of men and women, even those who are similarly educated. As various studies have shown, married women — even women with the best qualifications — are less likely than married men or unmarried women to succeed in the workplace.

Especially for women who choose a professional career, a tension exists between the kind of commitment one is supposed to make to a career and the commitment women are expected to make to family and children. Unfortunately for women, the prime years for starting a career — the years from 20 to 35 — are also the prime

years for starting a family. Women who leave the job market for any length of time during these years may find that they never catch up. Consequently, argue proponents of this third choice, if women are to combine child rearing and careers, high-quality infant and toddler care must be provided.

As things stand, professional women are often forced to make a choice. They can decide — in the words of a much-discussed article by Felice Schwartz, head of Catalyst, an organization devoted to advancing women's careers — to be "career-primary." That is, they can choose to remain single, or at least childless, in order to devote themselves to their careers. Or they

can choose the "mommy track." If they are willing to settle for less pay, less responsibility, and possibly a dead-end job, they will feel less pressure, be expected to work fewer hours, and be able to fill in from time to time when child care arrangements fall through.

The clamor over Schwartz's article underlined the inequity of the current situation: women are forced to make a choice that is rarely asked of men. Proponents of this third choice are convinced that a universal system of day care for preschoolers would reduce the strain felt by working mothers who have young children.

FIND YOUR WAR JOB
In Industry – Agriculture – Business

"I've found the job where I fit best!"

When women were needed in defense industries during the Second World War, the government provided day care facilities for their children.

In Canada, where the public day care system was recently expanded, one of the main arguments for doing so was that it would be a step toward equality between the sexes. In the words of Barbara McDougall, Canada's Minister for the Status of Women, "We regard child care as the key that opens the door to women's equality."

ALL HANDS ON DECK

Advocates of universal day care offer a final argument for universal day care. It is essential, they feel, to encourage women's participation in the labor force. In the words of economist Heidi Hartmann, director of the Institute for Women's Policy Research in Washington, "Policies that assist parents in combining work with family care — particularly child care services — help to ensure the availability of workers needed for future economic growth."

Considering the likelihood of labor shortages over the coming decade, that is no idle concern. Labor force experts anticipate shortages because the number of young adults age 16 - 24 is declining. Consequently, there will be relatively few of the people business relies on to fill entry-level jobs.

The combination of fewer workers and more available jobs is already evident in some sectors of the economy. Help-wanted signs dot suburban shopping malls, and corporate personnel officers have launched aggressive recruitment efforts to entice well-trained workers. These warning signs should be heeded, said Senator Edward Kennedy in January 1989, in congressional hearings on this topic. "Unless we act now, America will soon be without enough hands on deck to get the work of America done."

The Labor Department projects that over the next decade two out of three new jobs will be filled by women, most of whom are or will become mothers.

Consequently, women, who already make up about 45 percent of the labor force, will become an even more prominent economic resource. If the child care that working women desperately need is *not* provided, conclude proponents of this choice, it is likely to seriously impair America's future economic growth.

BLUEPRINT FOR CHILD CARE

Advocates of this choice conclude that child care is a necessity for families at all income levels. In the words of Alfred Kahn and Sheila Kamerman: "Child care should be regarded as neither a luxury nor a sometime thing for a few problem families. It is an essential component of community life. Child care is a matter of concern to a large proportion of families with children. It has major implications for the rearing of future generations, and thus for the well-being of our entire society."

Proponents of this choice insist that government as well as employers must invest additional resources to expand the supply and improve the quality of child care for families at all income levels. In their view, a comprehensive child care system should meet four criteria: availability, affordability, quality, and reliability.

To satisfy these criteria, say proponents of this choice, government should subsidize free or below-cost child care for which all children would be eligible. It should ensure that child care facilities meet certain standards regarding such considerations as safety, group size, and the training of professional staff. At the same time, employers should permit parents of young children more flexibility —

THE CORPORATE ROLE IN CHILD CARE

Every weekday morning, Diane Ronketty, an executive secretary at the Campbell Soup Company in Camden, New Jersey, drops her daughter Lisa at her day care center and then walks across the parking lot to her office. Usually, she stops in to see her daughter again at lunchtime, and then picks her up at the end of the workday. Lisa is enrolled in Campbell's on-site child care center, provided specifically for company employees.

As recently as 1982, only 600 American companies offered employees any kind of help with child care — either child care referral systems, financial assistance for parents who use child care, or on-site child care centers. Today, although on-site facilities such as the one at Campbell Soup are still the exception, at least 3,300 companies provide some kind of child care assistance.

- In some 250 communities across the country, IBM recruits and trains child care providers and operates a child care referral service.
- Stride Rite in Cambridge, Massachusetts is currently building an intergenerational center to help employees care for elderly relatives as well as young children.
- In Edison, New Jersey, the Heller Industrial Park offers a subsidized day care center whose services are available to town residents as well as employees of firms located in the industrial park.

Child care, says J. Douglass Phillips, director of corporate planning at Merck and Company, Inc., "is the sleeping giant of productivity improvement." Since so many mothers of young children are in the labor force, family obligations play a significant role in career decisions for men and women. Facing a declining labor force and an increasing need for female employees, many companies have begun to recognize that providing child care assistance is an effective way to attract new employees, and reduce employee turnover.

Employees whose young children are taken care of in on-site day care centers are reported to be less anxious. In the words of a single mother whose child attends the Campbell center, "Knowing you can get to your child in an emergency within minutes, and knowing you can see them if and when you want to during the day relieves a lot of tension and anxiety."

One of the benefits of on-site day care: a mid-day visit

Reportedly, on-site child care has also led to increased productivity. Researchers who studied corporate child care assistance programs found that since instituting such programs, most corporate personnel directors saw an improvement in employee morale, as well as less turnover and absenteeism. Virtually all of them concluded that the benefits of corporate child care programs outweigh the costs.

Many communities are considering new laws that would require employers and developers to help with child care. In Alameda County, California, for example, companies doing business with the county government are required by law to provide some sort of child care assistance to their employees. In San Francisco, developers of new office buildings and hotels are required to set aside 2,000 square feet for day care, or provide space for this purpose in a nearby facility.

With such examples in mind, some day care advocates have begun to lobby for federal laws that would require private companies to provide child care assistance. But opponents reply that the cost of doing so is substantial. Currently, the firms providing child care assistance are mainly large corporations, and unusually profitable ones. Smaller, less profitable companies might be unable to absorb the additional cost.

Critics conclude that the cost of this additional employee benefit would be taken out of wages, or it would cause employers to reduce other benefits such as health insurance or pension programs. Requiring employers to provide child care is discriminatory, say critics, since all workers end up subsidizing those with young children. Referring to the cost of providing child care assistance, Linda McFarland, a partner at Hewitt Associates, an employee benefit consulting firm, says that "family needs run up against the need to reduce costs."

Whether or not many communities follow the precedent of requiring employers to provide child care assistance, the corporate role in day care is likely to grow. But since so many working parents of young children are employed by small firms, this is at best a partial solution to the day care problem.

through flextime, and more generous parental leaves when babies are born — to make working and child rearing more compatible.

Advocates of such measures are quick to point out what they do *not* mean. They would not deny mothers who choose to stay home with their young children the right to do so. Neither would they call for a national network of government-run preschools. Instead, proponents would encourage as much diversity as is consistent with high standards.

To advocates of this solution to the child care dilemma, legislative proposals such as the Act for Better Child Care (ABC) represent a step in the right direction. The goal of the ABC bill — whose projected first-year price tag is $2.5 billion — is to encourage quality affordable child care by offering grants to child care providers ranging from church groups to public schools and family day care providers.

The bill would also establish a National Advisory Committee on Child Care to define minimum standards in such areas as teacher-student ratios, group size, and teacher training.

Providing day care subsidies for infants and preschoolers from families at all income levels would be an expensive proposition. Assuming that per child costs in day care centers and schools are roughly similar, and assuming that the children of most working parents would attend, the annual price tag of such subsidies would be about $30 billion. If child-staff ratios were lowered and licensing standards for facilities were raised, the cost would be even higher.

Advocates of this approach feel that, despite its high cost, it is an investment worth making. "We are spending billions of dollars," writes child care specialist Barry Brazelton, "to protect families from outside enemies, real and imagined. But we do not have

even 50 percent of the quality child care we need, and what we do have is neither affordable nor available to most families. By not facing the needs of families early on, we are endangering both the present and the future generation. Improving conditions for working parents has a visible payoff."

To reduce the cost of a comprehensive day care system, parents who can afford to do so could be asked to pay part of the cost. But, say proponents of this choice, no parent at any income level should be tempted to compromise for monetary reasons on the quality of their child's care.

"The bottom line," writes journalist Tony Schwartz, "is that our children are our future. We can only hope to get back from them as much as we put in. The first responsibility plainly is our own, as parents. But we must also create nourishing and nurturing environments for our children when we cannot be there. If we do not, we'll surely pay the price later on. Day care may not be appropriate for everyone. But it should be one of the available choices in a society that now offers working parents far too few."

WHAT CRITICS SAY

There is by no means a consensus that day care should be provided at public expense to all parents who want it. Nor is there general agreement that involving the government in day care to a much greater extent is a move in the right direction.

Some critics object to this approach on the grounds that it expands the federal education bureaucracy. The ABC bill, for example, would provide funds to the child care office within the Department of Health and Human Services. It would also require a variety of state panels and agencies to promulgate standards and regulations.

CAREER OPPORTUNITIES: MEN / WOMEN / WOMEN WITH CHILDREN — MIKE THOMPSON

> "We must move quickly to build a child care system that allows working families the peace of mind they need to be productive on their jobs."
> — Marian Wright Edelman

And government agencies would be involved in training administrators and establishing clearinghouses. It amounts, critics say, to the creation of a pediatric Pentagon, which is in no one's interest.

Other critics, who regard the issue from the perspective of the first choice we examined, reject the premises that child care is good for preschoolers, and that public policy should encourage women to enter the labor force. "Of course we should have a national child care policy," writes Phyllis Schlafly. "Our policy should be to encourage mothers to care for their own babies. If any subsidies are given, they should be given to promote mother care, not institutional care, for three reasons: it's better for babies, it's fairer to all Americans, and it's far less expensive."

Conceding that the effects of child care on preschoolers aren't clear, other critics are unconvinced that a comprehensive child care system would be a notable public good. In the words of columnist Robert Samuelson, "It's said that a federal system of child care, by helping our children, is an investment in our economic future. This is a seductive argument that seems sensible. Unfortunately, it probably isn't true."

In the words of child care expert Penelope Leach, "Most of a child's development takes place in the context of relationships with the people he or she cares about most deeply. Arranging life so that the child spends less time with those people, and more with others, is scarcely ever helpful to that child's development."

In any case, say critics of this choice, it is not a good idea for the government to encourage group care or to promote the illusion that doing so will relieve parental anxieties. Bearing

ARTHUR SIRDOFSKY, GAMMA/LIAISON

children and rearing them while carrying out other responsibilities is inherently stressful. But having children is a burden that is freely chosen, and one that brings considerable satisfaction.

A MATTER OF FAIRNESS

In particular, critics of this choice point to the inequities it creates. There is no reason, as they see it, why parents should not send a young child to day care while the mother works. Each family is free to make that decision. The problem with a system of universal day care provided at public expense is that it favors one way of raising children. In effect, the proposal for comprehensive day care assumes that mothers who work deserve help, while those who stay at home do not.

"No one has explained," writes David Kelley, "why it is fair to tax families in which the mother stays at home to support working parents, and especially two wage-earner families,

whose median income of $38,249 far exceeds the national average." Critics conclude that this amounts to an income redistribution plan that is blatantly unfair to families in which mothers choose to stay home, often at some financial sacrifice.

"The plight of the professional or business woman who wants someone else to provide her with a baby-sitter," writes Phyllis Schlafly, "should not be on any list of grievances for which someone else should provide a remedy. She has the income to buy her own domestic services, so she should cut out the crybaby act and stop asking others to subsidize the lifestyle she has chosen."

The child care debate comes down to differences about what is fair, differences about the role government should take, as well as differences about how to meet the needs of preschoolers and families — *all* families, not just the ones in which mothers work. ∎

PRESCRIPTION FOR PRESCHOOLERS: WHAT'S BEST FOR PARENTS AND CHILDREN

"The day care debate comes down to different views about what is fair and affordable, as well as differences about government's role, and how to meet the needs of preschoolers and their families."

As the 1980s come to a close, an unprecedented amount of legislative activity regarding child care is taking place in Washington and state capitals. Whether motivated by concern for the disadvantaged, concern about training the work force of the future, or relieving the stress experienced by working parents, child care proposals proliferate.

Some legislators propose public prekindergarten programs for 3- and 4-year-olds, all-day programs for 5-year-olds, and the creation of more day care centers, especially facilities that provide infant care. Others favor tax breaks for families with young children to encourage full-time maternal care. Proposals that encourage employers to offer longer parental leave and provide on-site day care are particularly popular.

Most legislators — and most of the American public — agree with President Bush's assertion that the states and the federal government should provide additional resources to help solve the problem. However, there are real differences, as we have seen, about what kind of assistance should be offered.

Media coverage of the day care debate has focused on the details of various proposals, such as the Bush administration's plan to provide up to $1,000 in tax credits for each child under the age of 4 for about 2.5 million low-income families — a credit that would be refundable, so that families who pay no income taxes could still receive assistance. The chief alternative proposal under consideration in Washington early in 1989 was a more comprehensive measure, the ABC bill, which would provide direct subsidies to child care providers serving low-income families, while strengthening standards for child care facilities.

These proposals raise dozens of questions, some of them quite specific: Is it a good idea, as the ABC bill specifies, to offer funding to non-sectarian church-sponsored preschools, or does that violate the principle of church-state separation? The Bush tax credit proposal raises questions about how much assistance is enough. "To propose a $1,000 federal tax credit and call it child care is misleading," said Senator Christopher Dodd. "Twenty dollars a week to a struggling family that needs child care is not what I call help."

Media accounts of the day care debate typically feature the cost of various child care proposals. Reporters have repeatedly speculated that, in the shadow of a towering deficit, members of Congress are unlikely to approve new spending proposals for child care, no matter how commendable their purpose.

WAYS AND MEANS

In an important respect, choosing among child care initiatives is a budgetary matter that forces us to weigh the importance of child care against other needs, and to balance the cost of programs in this area against other public commitments.

The cost of the Administration's tax credit proposal — generally favored by proponents of our first choice as a way of relieving the tax burden for poor parents — is estimated to be about $2.5 billion per year. Even this measure, which critics regard as too modest to make much of a difference, would add substantially to the cost of the existing child care tax credit, which is about $4 billion.

Providing a more generous tax credit to *all* parents of children under age 6, not just to poor parents or to those who use organized day care, would be more costly. If, as Allan Carlson proposes, we encouraged mothers of young children to stay home by raising the tax exemption for each child under 6 from $2,000 to $4,000, it would cost $40 billion per year.

In comparison, proponents of the second choice favor expanding the Head Start program five-fold, so that virtually all 3- and 4-year-old children from low-income families who qualify could attend such programs. It would cost roughly $5 billion. Proponents of this choice also favor other forms of child care assistance to low-income families.

The cost of providing public subsidies for a comprehensive day care system, as proposed in our third choice, would be substantially higher. The ABC bill, which represents a step in that direction, carries a first-year price tag of $2.5 billion, and authorizes "such sums as may be necessary" for future years. Since about 10 million children under age 6 have mothers in the labor force, and the per child cost of providing such care is roughly $3,000 per year, the cost of free public day care for all preschoolers whose parents want to use it would be approximately $30 billion. That is more than the annual budget of the Department of Education, and roughly twice the amount spent on Aid to Families with Dependent Children, the federal-state program of cash assistance to the poor.

Confronted with the stark reality of the deficit, proponents of various child care proposals have tried to minimize the cost of their proposed expenditures by depicting them as invest-

ments that will yield future dividends, such as contributing to a better-educated and more productive labor force. Still, as House minority leader Robert Michel put it, "Spending is spending, regardless of how one tries to explain it away."

The question is whether many people's eagerness to expand the public role in assisting families with young children is matched by their willingness to pay for it. Special taxes earmarked for children's programs are already being discussed. In Florida, a new law allows counties to levy special property taxes for children's programs. In the state of Washington, a campaign is under way to put a "children's initiative" on the ballot, and to levy new taxes to the amount of $360 million for children's programs.

In general, the American public strongly opposes higher taxes. But perhaps in this instance people feel so strongly about the need for new programs that they are willing to pay more to get them. Several polls,

including a 1986 Harris poll, show that a majority of Americans say they *would* be willing to pay more taxes for day care programs.

In this respect, the central issue in the day care debate is whether the need for a government role is so compelling as to justify major new expenditures — and the additional taxes needed to pay for them.

GOALS OF PUBLIC ACTION

In a broader sense, preoccupation with the details of various child care proposals and their cost obscures the central questions in the day care debate. Before legislators can choose among various day care proposals, they need to know how most Americans feel about moving in one direction rather than another.

A fundamental question in the child care debate is whether we can reach a consensus about which arrangements are in the best interest of the nation's preschoolers — not just the 10.5

million children under age 6 whose mothers are in the labor force, but all 20 million preschoolers.

As W. Norton Grubb, an economist at the University of California at Berkeley, points out, the debate about whether publicly subsidized facilities should be offered to younger children has been going on for 150 years. Over that period, the terms of the debate have changed very little.

"The proposal to extend schooling to younger children," writes Grubb, "is an idea that every generation seems to rediscover for itself. This idea has been prompted by different motives — in turn educational, economic, and reformist, sometimes stressing the needs of children and sometimes forgetting the child in favor of social problems."

The chief questions, then and now, are whether child care for young children is good for them, and whether it is a public good. With regard to preschoolers as well as school-age children in the nineteenth century, writes Grubb, "education was deemed particularly important for poor children, whose parents, according to contemporary sources, 'seldom kept any government in their families' and who therefore 'unavoidably contracted habits of idleness, mischief, and wickedness.'"

The infant school movement, most active in the 1830s and 1840s, was a precursor to the position advocated in the second choice, which insists that preschools are a public obligation only for children from disadvantaged families. As Grubb notes, the vision of the infant school movement — that preschool facilities should be provided for children from "bad homes" to teach them and compensate for early deficiencies — is reflected in the current interest in early education for the disadvantaged.

Though it focused on the needs of children from poor families, the infant school movement stimulated broad interest in early childhood education, and it spawned infant schools for children from middle-class families. By the mid-nineteenth century, however, interest in infant schools subsided as the view that mothers should care for their own children became more influential.

Today, this view remains influential. As we saw in choice one, some parents and child development specialists contend that a substantial amount of nonparental care poses a serious risk for young children, particularly for infants. From this perspective, the chief question that should be asked of proposals that purport to help young children is whether they help the family perform its functions — or whether they substitute government-subsidized care performed by others. The best thing government can do for families, say proponents of that choice, is to relieve their tax burden. "The central lesson of the last 100 years," writes Allan Carlson, "is that the state can disrupt, but it cannot save families."

In contrast, advocates of our third choice conclude that since family life has changed decisively — particularly because of the influx of mothers into the labor force — it is time to define preschool care as a public responsibility. From this perspective, to insist upon full-time maternal care is to indulge in nostalgia. Child care policy, says human development expert Alison Clarke-Stewart, must "proceed from reality. Maternal employment is a reality. The issue today, therefore, is not *whether* infants should be in day care but *how* to make their experiences there and at home supportive of their development and of their parents' peace of mind."

WHAT'S FAIR

Finally, the day care debate is about what is fair. Proponents of day care for the disadvantaged feel that it is unfair not to make day care available to young children from poor families. In the words of David Hamburg, president of the Carnegie Corporation, "It's a question of equity. Middle-class parents are already giving their children these benefits."

Those who favor universal day care feel that it is unfair to expect women to work as men's equal in the workplace as long as they are obliged to bear most of the burden of caring for preschool children. That is one reason why proponents of our third choice insist that parents at all income levels need affordable, publicly subsidized day care.

To proponents of our first choice, providing day care as a publicly subsidized activity is manifestly unfair, since it amounts to a form of discrimination against families in which the mothers stay home to care for young children.

No child care policy will be regarded universally as fair. The point is to recognize various views about what's fair, and to decide which inequities *must* be remedied.

Traditionally, says political scientist Ethel Klein, "Americans have been reluctant to acknowledge that government has any role or responsibility for young children, particularly children who don't come from poor families." The question is whether a new consensus has emerged, which supports a clearly defined government role in helping parents take care of preschool children. The central issue, says Dana E. Friedman, founder of the Families and Work Institute, "is when personal problems become a public responsibility." ■

For Further Reading

For a statistical profile of child care arrangements, see *Who's Minding the Kids: Child Care Arrangements,* Winter 1984-1985, United States Department of Commerce, Bureau of the Census, P-70, No. 9, May 1987. The Congressional Research Service has prepared a useful overview, written by Thomas Gabe and Sharon Stephan, entitled *Child Day Care: Patterns of Use Among Families with Preschool Children,* December, 1988.

For a historical perspective, see Margaret O'Brien Steinfels, *Who's Minding the Children? The History and Politics of Day Care in America* (New York: Simon and Schuster, 1973). W. Norton Grubb compares current child care proposals to earlier efforts, and lays out the choices facing the states in *Young Children Face the States: Issues and Options for Early Childhood Programs* (New Brunswick, NJ: Eagleton Institute of Politics, 1987).

Alfred Kahn and Sheila Kamerman review the child care issue, covering such topics as trends in child care, local and state actions, and the role of employers and schools, in *Child Care: Facing the Hard Choices* (Dover, MA: Auburn House Publishing Co., 1987).

Several articles in the February 1989 issue of *American Psychologist* summarize and assess the literature on the effects of day care. In particular, see K. Alison Clarke-Stewart's "Infant Day Care: Maligned or Malignant?" and Ron Haskins' "Beyond Metaphor: The Efficacy of Early Childhood Education."

For a review of current federal involvements in child care and their cost, see Douglas Besharov and Paul Tramontozzi, *The Cost of Federal Child Care Assistance* (Washington, DC:

ROB SAUNDERS

American Enterprise Institute, 1988). A report from the Congressional Research Service, *Child Day Care: Summaries of Selected Major Bills in the 100th Congress,* prepared by Sharon Stephan, Karen Spar, and Anne Stewart, (Washington, DC: C.R.S., October, 1988) provides a guide to legislative proposals.

The Eagle Forum, a group that lobbies against child care for preschoolers, has published an anthology reflecting the arguments presented in our first choice. See *Who Will Rock the Cradle?* edited by Phyllis Schlafly (Alton, IL: Eagle Forum, 1989). William Dreskin and Wendy Dreskin review the arguments against full day care in *The Day Care Decision: What's Best for You and Your Child* (New York: M. Evans, 1983). For an assessment of the literature on mother-child attachment, particularly John Bowlby's work, see Bob Mullan's *Are Mothers Really Necessary?* (NY: Weidenfeld & Nicolson, 1988).

On child care for the disadvantaged, see Edward Zigler and Jeanette Valentine, eds., *Project Head Start: A Legacy of the War on Poverty* (New York: Free Press, 1979). For a report on the long-term effects of the Perry Preschool Program, see John Berrueta-Clement, et al., *Changed Lives: The Effects of the Perry Preschool*

Program on Youths Through Age 19 (Ypsilanti, MI: High/Scope Press, 1984). Enid Borden and Kate Walsh O'Beirne raise questions about the long-term effects of such programs in "False Start? The Fleeting Gains at Head Start," *Policy Review* (Winter 1989).

For a summary of relevant trends, and an argument for a comprehensive child care policy, see the Child Care Action Campaign's report, *Child Care: The Bottom Line* by Barbara Reisman, et al. (New York: CCAC, 1988).

Acknowledgments

Many people participated in the process of deciding upon this year's topics, discussing how they should be approached, and preparing the materials. Once again this year, David Mathews and Daniel Yankelovich provided both guidance and support. Jon Rye Kinghorn played a vital role in providing assistance to the convening institutions and Forum leaders.

For their advice and assistance in sharpening the arguments contained in this booklet, we are grateful to Douglas Besharov, resident scholar at the American Enterprise Institute and Dana Friedman, founder of the Families and Work Institute. In addition, our colleagues John Doble, Jean Johnson, Jon Rye Kinghorn, Robert Kingston, Suzanne Morse, Pat Scully, Jeffrey Tuchman, and Deborah Wadsworth helped to refine the framework and to clarify the argument.

Finally, we would like to thank Joan Marlatt and the Children's Workroom for providing a photo opportunity. A special note of appreciation to Alison Melville for her assistance and enthusiasm about the project.

NATIONAL ISSUES FORUMS

The National Issues Forums (NIF) program consists of locally initiated Forums and study circles which bring citizens together in communities throughout the nation for nonpartisan discussions about public issues. In these Forums, the traditional town meeting concept is re-created. Each fall and winter, three issues of particular concern are addressed in these groups. The results are then shared with policymakers.

More than a thousand civic and education organizations — high schools and colleges, libraries, service organizations, religious groups, and other types of groups — convene Forums and study circles in their communities as part of the National Issues Forums. Each participating organization assumes ownership of the program, adapting the NIF approach and materials to its own mission and to the needs of the local community. In this sense, there is no one type of NIF program. There are many varieties, all locally directed and financed.

Here are answers to some of the most frequently asked questions about the National Issues Forums:

"WHAT HAPPENS IN FORUMS?"

The goal of Forums and study circles is to stimulate and sustain a certain kind of conversation — a genuinely useful conversation that moves beyond the bounds of partisan politics and the airing of grievances to mutually acceptable responses to common problems. Distinctively, Forums invite discussion about each of several choices, along with their cost and the main arguments for and against them. Forum moderators encourage participants to examine their values and preferences — as individuals and as community members — and apply them to specific issues.

"CAN I PARTICIPATE IF I'M NOT WELL INFORMED ABOUT THE ISSUE?"

To discuss public issues, citizens need to grasp the underlying problem or dilemma, and they should understand certain basic facts and trends. But it isn't necessary to know a great deal about an issue. NIF discussions focus on what public actions should be taken. That's a matter of judgment that requires collective deliberation. The most important thing to ponder and discuss is the kernel of convictions on which each alternative is based. The task of the National Issues Forums is not to help participants acquire a detailed knowledge of the issue but to help people sort out conflicting principles and preferences, to find out where they agree and disagree and work toward common understandings.

"ISN'T ONE PERSON'S OPINION AS GOOD AS ANOTHER'S?"

Public judgment differs from personal opinion. It arises when people sort out their values and work through hard choices. Public judgment reflects people's views once they have an opportunity to confront an issue seriously, consider the arguments for and against various positions, and come to terms with the consequences of their beliefs.

"ARE FORUM PARTICIPANTS EXPECTED TO AGREE UPON A COURSE OF ACTION?"

A fundamental challenge in a democratic nation is sustaining a consensus about a broad direction of public action without ignoring or denying the diversity of individual preferences. Forums do not attempt to achieve complete agreement. Rather, their goal is to help people see which interests are shareable and which are not. A Forum moderator once described the common ground in these words: "Here are five statements that were made in our community Forum. Not everyone agreed with all of them. But there is nothing in them that we couldn't agree with."

"WHAT'S THE POINT OF ONE MORE BULL SESSION?"

Making choices is hard work. It requires something more than talking about public issues. "Talking about" is what we do every day. We talk about the weather, or our friends, or the government. But the "choice work" that takes place in Forum discussions involves weighing alternatives and considering the consequences of various courses of action. It means accepting certain choices even if they aren't entirely consistent with what we want, and even if the cost is higher than we imagined. Forum participants learn how to work through issues together. That means using talk to discover, not just to persuade or advocate.

"DO THE FORUMS LEAD TO POLITICAL ACTION?"

Neither local convenors nor the National Issues Forums as a whole advocate partisan positions or specific solutions. The Forums' purpose is to influence the political process in a more fundamental way. Before elected officials decide upon specific proposals, they need to know what kinds of initiatives the public favors. As President Carter once said, "Government cannot set our goals and it cannot define our vision." The purpose of the Forums is to provide an occasion for people to decide what broad direction public action should take.

PRE-FORUM BALLOT

THE DAY CARE DILEMMA:
WHO SHOULD BE RESPONSIBLE FOR THE CHILDREN?

One of the reasons people participate in the National Issues Forums is that they want leaders to know how they feel about the issues. So that we can present your thoughts and feelings about this issue, we'd like you to fill out this ballot before you attend Forum meetings (or before you read this book, if you buy it elsewhere), and a second ballot after the Forum (or after you've read the material).

The moderator of your local Forum will ask you to hand in this ballot at the end of the session. If you cannot attend the meeting, send the completed ballot to National Issues Forums, 100 Commons Road, Dayton, Ohio 45459-2777.

1. Please indicate how you feel about the following approaches to child care.

		Agree	**Disagree**	**Not Sure**
a.	The government should offer financial incentives to encourage mothers to stay home and care for their preschool children.	☐	☐	☐
b.	The government should offer child care assistance to all low-income families with preschool children.	☐	☐	☐
c.	The government should subsidize high-quality child care for *all* preschool children, regardless of family income.	☐	☐	☐
d.	We cannot afford to increase government spending for child care at this time.	☐	☐	☐
e.	Corporations should be required to provide child care assistance to their employees.	☐	☐	☐
f.	Corporations should be required to offer job-protected parental leaves to employees who want to spend time with their infants.	☐	☐	☐

2. What is your reaction to the following statements about child care?

		Agree	**Disagree**	**Not Sure**
a.	Whenever possible, infants and children under 2 should be cared for exclusively by their mothers.	☐	☐	☐
b.	Whenever possible, children between the ages of 2 and 5 should be cared for exclusively by their mothers.	☐	☐	☐
c.	Encouraging mothers to stay home and care for their own children strengthens the family unit.	☐	☐	☐
d.	Most mothers would prefer to stay home and care for their own children but they cannot currently afford to do so.	☐	☐	☐
e.	Most women want to have both children *and* a career.	☐	☐	☐
f.	Many low-income mothers need child care assistance so that they can get off welfare and go to work.	☐	☐	☐
g.	Child care programs, such as Head Start, help poor preschool children do better in school and eventually break out of a cycle of poverty.	☐	☐	☐

NATIONAL ISSUES FORUMS

(over)

	Agree	Disagree	Not Sure
h. There is an absence of high-quality, affordable child care not just for children from poor families, but for *all* children.	☐	☐	☐
i. Preschool children from all types of families would benefit from subsidized child care programs.	☐	☐	☐
j. Universal child care is needed to help parents balance family and work demands.	☐	☐	☐
k. We should encourage more women to enter the work force in the future.	☐	☐	☐
l. Child care should be regarded as a public good, much like roads or schools, that will not be adequately provided unless the government takes responsibility for it.	☐	☐	☐
m. Child care is a personal problem that each family should deal with on its own.	☐	☐	☐

---

3. Which of these age groups are you in?

☐ Under 18 ☐ 18-29 ☐ 30-44 ☐ 45-64 ☐ Over 65

---

4. Are you a ☐ Man ☐ Woman

---

5. What is your ZIP code? _____

THE DAY CARE DILEMMA:
WHO SHOULD BE RESPONSIBLE FOR THE CHILDREN?

Now that you've had a chance to read the book or attend a Forum discussion we'd like to know what you think about this issue. Your opinions, along with those of thousands of others who participated in this year's Forums, will be reflected in a summary report prepared for participants as well as elected officials and policymakers working on this problem. Since we're interested in whether you have changed your mind about certain aspects of this issue, the questions are the same as those you answered earlier.

Please hand this ballot to the Forum leader at the end of the session, or mail it to National Issues Forums, 100 Commons Road, Dayton, Ohio 45459-2777.

---

1. Please indicate how you feel about the following approaches to child care.

	Agree	Disagree	Not Sure
a. The government should offer financial incentives to encourage mothers to stay home and care for their preschool children.	☐	☐	☐
b. The government should offer child care assistance to all low-income families with preschool children.	☐	☐	☐
c. The government should subsidize high-quality child care for *all* preschool children, regardless of family income.	☐	☐	☐
d. We cannot afford to increase government spending for child care at this time.	☐	☐	☐
e. Corporations should be required to provide child care assistance to their employees.	☐	☐	☐
f. Corporations should be required to offer job-protected parental leaves to employees who want to spend time with their infants.	☐	☐	☐

---

2. What is your reaction to the following statements about child care?

	Agree	Disagree	Not Sure
a. Whenever possible, infants and children under 2 should be cared for exclusively by their mothers.	☐	☐	☐
b. Whenever possible, children between the ages of 2 and 5 should be cared for exclusively by their mothers.	☐	☐	☐
c. Encouraging mothers to stay home and care for their own children strengthens the family unit.	☐	☐	☐
d. Most mothers would prefer to stay home and care for their own children but they cannot currently afford to do so.	☐	☐	☐
e. Most women want to have both children *and* a career.	☐	☐	☐
f. Many low-income mothers need child care assistance so that they can get off welfare and go to work.	☐	☐	☐

		Agree	Disagree	Not Sure
g.	Child care programs, such as Head Start, help poor preschool children do better in school and eventually break out of a cycle of poverty.	☐	☐	☐
h.	There is an absence of high-quality, affordable child care not just for children from poor families, but for *all* children.	☐	☐	☐
i.	Preschool children from all types of families would benefit from subsidized child care programs.	☐	☐	☐
j.	Universal child care is needed to help parents balance family and work demands.	☐	☐	☐
k.	We should encourage more women to enter the work force in the future.	☐	☐	☐
l.	Child care should be regarded as a public good, much like roads or schools, that will not be adequately provided unless the government takes responsibility for it.	☐	☐	☐
m.	Child care is a personal problem that each family should deal with on its own.	☐	☐	☐

---

3. Which of these age groups are you in?

☐ Under 18   ☐ 18-29   ☐ 30-44   ☐ 45-64   ☐ Over 65

---

4. Are you a   ☐ Man   ☐ Woman

---

5. What is your ZIP code? _____

---

6. We'd like to know whether, as you read this book and attended the Forums, you changed your mind about who should be responsible for caring for the nation's children. How, if at all, did you change your mind?

---

7. If there were just one message you could send to elected leaders on the topic of child care, what would it be?